ADVENTURE BEGINS HERE!

EXPLORE!
WORKBOOK

ages 4–5

PRE-K
pre-kindergarten

National Geographic
Washington, D.C.

This book belongs to:

First Name:

Last Name:

Since 1888, the National Geographic Society has funded more than 14,000 research, conservation, education, and storytelling projects around the world. National Geographic Partners distributes a portion of the funds it receives from your purchase to National Geographic Society to support programs including the conservation of animals and their habitats. To learn more, visit natgeo.com/info.

For more information, visit nationalgeographic.com, call 1-877-873-6846, or write to the following address:

National Geographic Partners, LLC
1145 17th Street NW
Washington, DC 20036-4688 U.S.A.

More for kids from National Geographic:
natgeokids.com

National Geographic Kids magazine inspires children to explore their world with fun yet educational articles on animals, science, nature, and more. Using fresh storytelling and amazing photography, *Nat Geo Kids* shows kids ages 6 to 14 the fascinating truth about the world—and why they should care. natgeo.com/subscribe

For rights or permissions inquiries, please contact National Geographic Books Subsidiary Rights: bookrights@natgeo.com

Cover design by Eva Absher-Schantz
Cover illustration by Melanie Mikecz
Interior illustration by Six Red Marbles

Trade paperback ISBN: 978-1-4263-7676-4

The publisher would like to thank Dr. Jan Esteraich, expert reviewer, and Katherine Kling, fact-checker. Book team: Katharine Moore, senior editor; Lori Epstein, photo manager; Six Red Marbles, writing, fact-checking, production; and Lauren Sciortino and David Marvin, associate designers.

Printed in China
24/RRDH/1

Dear Parents and Caregivers,

These interactive pages teach the academic skills kids need to succeed in pre-K, while focusing on favorite topics that will keep them engaged and excited as they learn. In these chapters, we explore themes associated with the natural world and everyday life, from forests and farms to weather, space, and community. Your child will be introduced to the most common preschool academic standards in true Nat Geo Kids style: through bold photos of nature, fun facts, jokes, and more.

To use this book, read through each theme-based spread with your child. Work with them to answer the questions and, as they progress, encourage independent problem-solving. Kid-friendly activities, such as connect the dots, mazes, and matching, make learning fun. Drawing, coloring, and writing activities help refine your child's fine motor skills. Each chapter covers the different content areas and early concepts your child will encounter at school, from math, reading, and writing to sorting, colors, and the natural sciences. This integrated approach exposes your child to STEM concepts across multiple curriculum subjects, laying the groundwork for a lifelong love of science and exploration.

You can do the activities in any order you choose. If you go in order, your child will be introduced to the letters of the alphabet and numbers 1 through 10 in the first few chapters. As you do each activity, notice the skill label listed above it. If you feel your child needs more practice with a particular skill, visit the skills index at the back of the book on pages 251–252. It lists all the activities where you can practice that skill with your child. It organizes the activities by skill, such as letters, math, reading, writing, and early concepts.

At the end of each chapter, your child has a chance to reflect on their learning and take part in fun drawing, coloring, and counting activities. Once your child completes all the chapters, you can celebrate their accomplishment by awarding them the certificate at the end of the book. Together, you'll explore a great big world of learning!

Table of Contents

CHAPTER 1

An owl can turn its head almost all the way around in either direction!

Forest Friends

It's time for a nature hike!

Let's find out about the animals and plants that live in the forest. In this chapter, keep a lookout for a forest friend you'd like to learn more about.

Red pandas have fluffy tails. They use their tails as blankets when it gets cold!

An Apple a Day

Q Why did the tree take a nap? →

There are many different kinds of trees. Some trees grow fruit, like apples. Do you like to eat apples?

EARLY CONCEPTS

Where's the Fruit?

Apples take time to grow.

Which tree has apples? Circle it.

LETTERS **WRITING**

A is for Apple

Trace and then write **A** and **a**. What sound does this letter make?

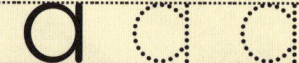

A A A

a a a

Pick a Snack

Count the number of apples in the basket.

A For rest!

There is 1! Trace and then write the number 1.

Colorful Apples

Apples can be different colors.

Color one apple red, one green, and one yellow. Circle your favorite color of apple!

So Many Animals!

Many animals live in the forest. You'll find them climbing in the trees, walking on the ground, and flying through the air!

EARLY CONCEPTS **MATH**

A Wooded Walk

Help the raccoon find its den before morning. Follow the dashed line to complete the maze. Look closely! The path through the forest makes the number 2.

Raccoons sleep in their dens during the day. They come out to explore at night.

LETTERS WRITING

B is for Bear

Bear cubs stay with their mom for up to three years!

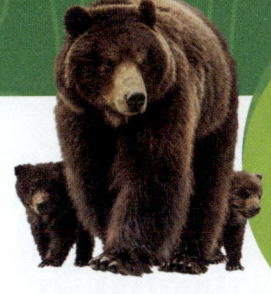

Trace and then write B and b. What sound does this letter make?

B B B

b b b

MATH WRITING

Out on a Limb

How many owls are on the branch?

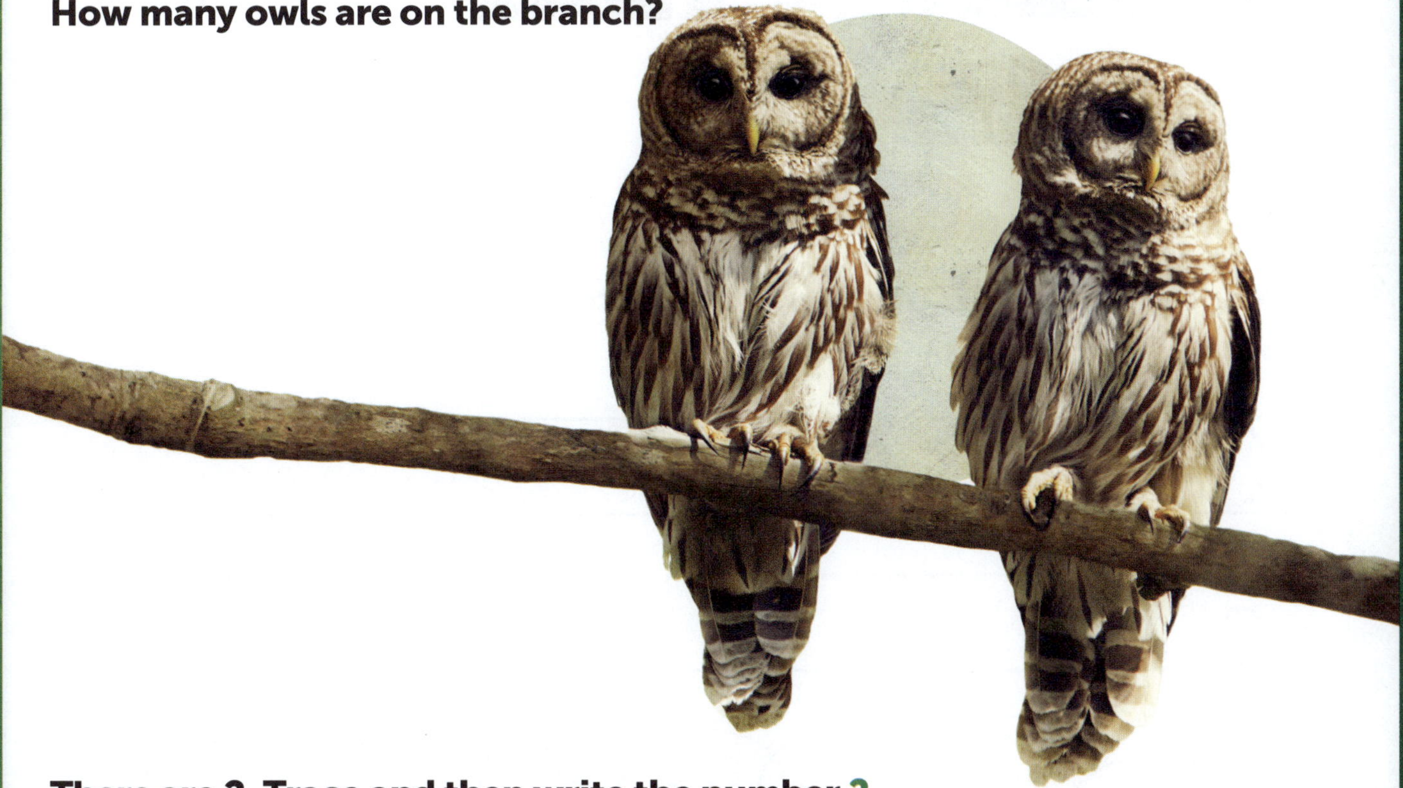

There are 2. Trace and then write the number 2.

2 2 2

Crawly Caterpillars

A caterpillar can be fuzzy, smooth, or spiky. One day it will turn into a butterfly or a moth!

A Wiggly Pattern

Look at the pattern. Circle the caterpillar that comes next.

LETTERS **WRITING**

C is for Caterpillar

Color the caterpillar. Trace and then write C and c. What sound does this letter make?

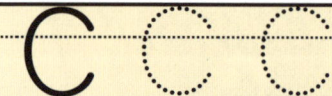

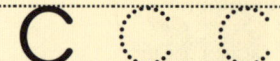

Counting Crawlers

How many crawling caterpillars do you see?
Circle the correct number. Then color them in!

2   3   4

Growing caterpillars spend most of their time munching on plants.

You counted 3 crawling caterpillars.

Trace and then write the number 3.

3 3 3

Home Sweet Home

Some animals live in a home called a den. Foxes dig a den in the ground. The den keeps them safe.

MATH **WRITING**

How Many Foxes?

Count the foxes in the den. Circle the correct number.

2   3   4

You counted 4 foxes. Trace and then write the number 4.

4 4 4

D is for Den

Trace and then write **D** and **d**. What sound does this letter make?

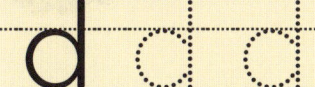

EARLY CONCEPTS

Go Home, Mama!

Other animals live in dens, too.

Draw a line to help each mom get home to her babies.

Soaring Eagles

Eagles use their large, powerful wings to soar high in the sky. They can spot food from very far away.

Where's the Eagle?

Draw an eagle flying over the tree.

Draw an eagle flying under the tree branches.

A Tasty Meal

Bald eagles like to eat fish.

Circle 5 fish.

You circled 5 fish. Trace and then write the number 5.

5 5 5

The eagle ate _____ fish.

E is for Eagle

A bald eagle's wings can reach seven feet (2 m) from end to end. That's about the height of a doorway.

Trace and then write E and e. What sound does this letter make?

E E E

e e e

A Growing Forest

A forest is made up of lots of trees and other plants. Those plants need water and sunlight to grow.

Plant Needs

A sapling is a young tree.

Draw lines from the sapling to the things it needs to grow.

Forest Flowers

Flowers make seeds so that new plants can grow.

How many wildflowers do you see? Write the number of flowers in the box below, and then color the picture!

_____ flowers

Trace and then write the number 6.

6 6 6

LETTERS | WRITING

F is for Forest

Trace and then write F and f. What sound does this letter make?

F F F

f f f

Furry Groundhogs

Groundhogs are great climbers and swimmers!
They live in burrows, or tunnels in the ground.

LETTERS **WRITING**

G is for Groundhog

Groundhogs are furry creatures!

Trace and then write G and g. What sound does this letter make?

G G G

g g g

EARLY CONCEPTS **MATH** **WRITING**

Who Looks the Same?

Circle the 2 groundhogs that are the same. Count them all and write the number!

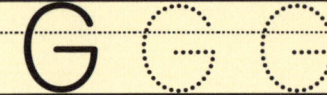

There are _____ groundhogs.

You counted 7 groundhogs. Trace and then write the number 7.

7 7 7

Back to the Burrow

Do you see the leaves below? Which leaf is first? Which is next? Which is last? This is a pattern. Follow the pattern through the burrow to help the groundhog find its family!

Happy Habitats

A habitat is where a plant or an animal lives. Can you think of some animals that live in a forest habitat?

LETTERS

Hiding in the Forest

A forest habitat is full of good hiding places.

Can you find the hidden letter H in the picture? Color it.

LETTERS **WRITING**

H is for Habitat

Trace and then write H and h. What sound does this letter make?

On the Run

Help the ant run across the colorful leaves!

Which number is missing from the leaves? Write the number.

Ants live in almost every habitat on Earth.

1

2

3

5

4

6

7

Trace and then write the number 8.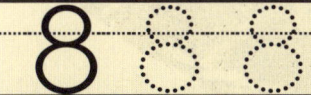

8 8 8

Inside the Lodge

Beavers build their homes, called lodges, in water.
They build them out of branches, mud, and rocks.

EARLY CONCEPTS

What's in a Lodge?

Which of these items does a beaver use to build its lodge? Draw a line from those objects to the lodge.

A Beaver Builds

Start building, beaver! Count the logs the beaver will add to its lodge.

The beaver will add _____ logs to the lodge.

Trace and then write the number 9.

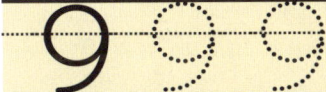

I is for Inside

The beaver sleeps and eats inside the lodge.

Trace and then write I and i. What sound does this letter make?

Beavers can cut down trees with their teeth!

Jump, Deer!

Deer are great jumpers! They can jump high to reach food or leap over logs and fences.

Growing Up

Baby deer eat leaves, seeds, and grass to grow strong.

Circle the smallest deer. Draw an X on the largest deer.

Baby deer are called fawns.

LETTERS **WRITING**

J is for Jump

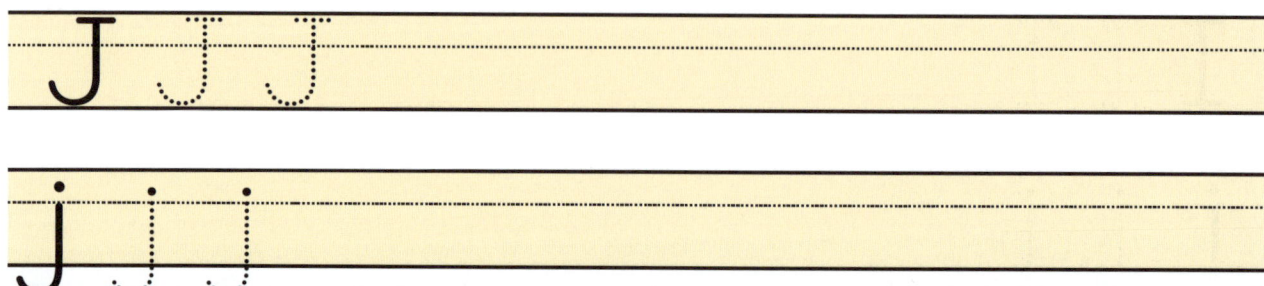

Trace and then write **J** and **j**. What sound does this letter make?

J J J

j j j

Count the Deer

Count the jumping deer.

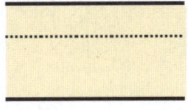

There are _____ jumping deer.

Trace and then write the number 10.

10 10 10

Good Night, Forest

It's almost nighttime in the forest! Some forest creatures are on their way to sleep, and others are just waking up to spend the night looking for food. What's one thing you learned about forests?

EARLY CONCEPTS **MATH**

Forest Pals

Add your favorite forest animal to the picture. Then count all the animals on both pages and write the number.

There are [ ] animals in the forest.

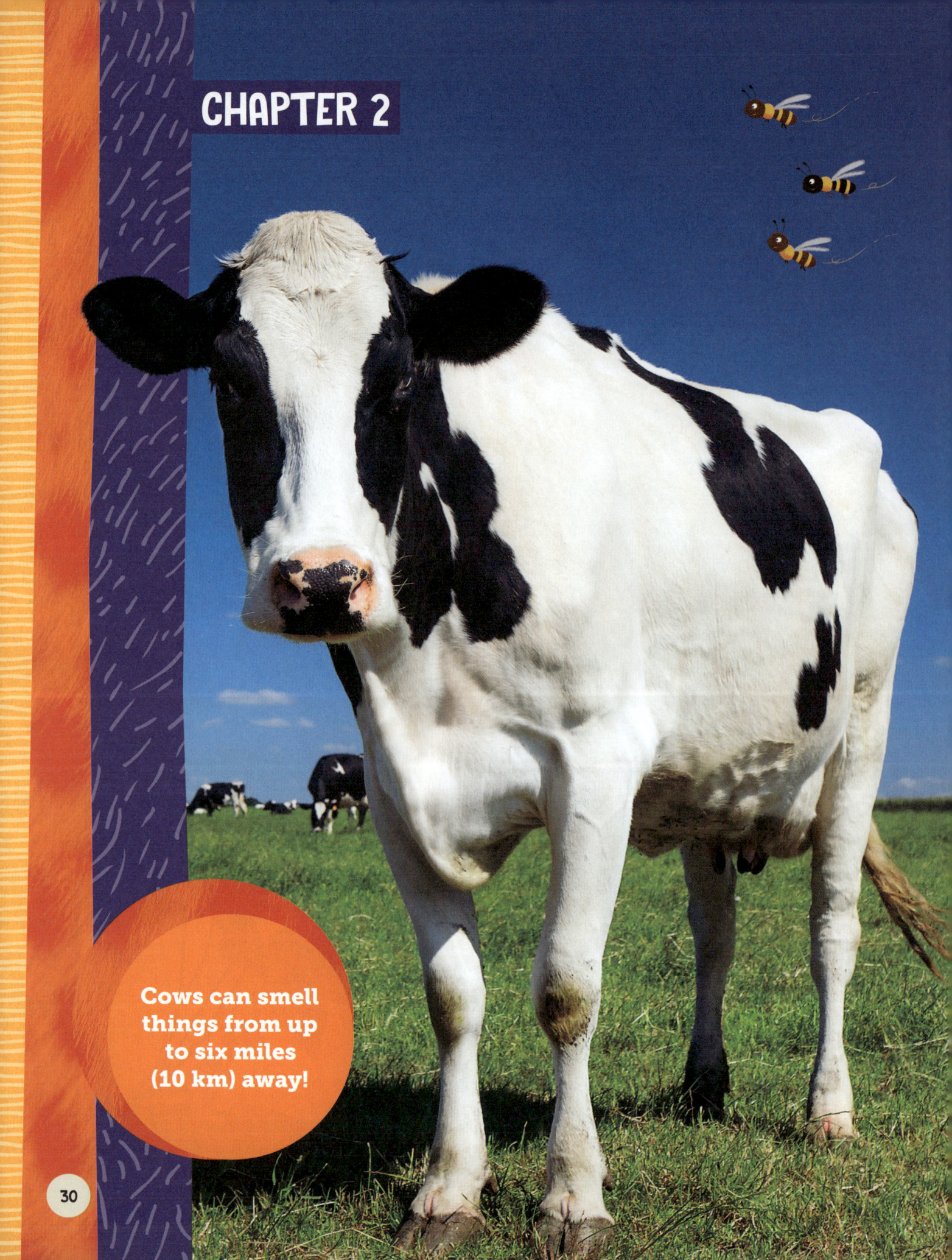

CHAPTER 2

Cows can smell things from up to six miles (10 km) away!

On the Farm

Let's take a trip to the farm!

On farms, people grow plants and care for animals. Turn the page to *moooooove* along to the barn!

? What would you grow if you were a farmer?

In the Barn

Many farms have a big building called a barn. A barn can hold tools and vehicles. Farm animals may live in a barn.

LETTERS   **WRITING**

K is for Kitten

A kitten can make its home in a barn.

Trace and then write K and k. What sound does this letter make?

MATH

More Hay, Please!

How many bales of hay does the farmer have? He wants to have 10. Draw what the farmer is missing.

Help Us Get Home

Uh-oh! The animals got lost!

Trace the lines to help the animals get back to the barn.

? If you were a farmer, what animals would you keep on your farm?

Little Lambs

Lambs are baby sheep. They live with other sheep in a group called a flock. Lambs can remember people they meet!

EARLY CONCEPTS | **LETTERS**

Lamb Matchup

First, point to the lambs that match. Then circle the 2 lambs that show the same letter.

LETTERS | **WRITING**

L is for Lamb

Trace and then write L and l. What sound does this letter make?

Circles Everywhere

This lamb has a circle on its collar.

Can you find other circles in the picture? Color them.

Dairy Farm

Female cows make milk. Farmers collect the milk for people to drink. Farms where cows make milk are called dairy farms.

LETTERS **WRITING**

M is for Milk

Trace and then write M and m. What sound does this letter make?

M M M M

m m m m

MATH

Milk to Share

The cow made lots of fresh milk!

Count how many glasses. Circle the correct number.

6   7   8

Back to the Barn

Help the cow find its food! Follow a path through the maze.

Most cows make more than six gallons (23 L) of milk each day!

Let's Eat!

What do farm animals eat? One important food is hay.
Farmers dry green plants to make hay for the animals.

Q What did the fast egg say to the slow egg?

LETTERS | **WRITING**

N is for Nutrients

Nutrients are all the things in food that help people and animals grow strong.

Trace and then write N and n. What sound does this letter make?

EARLY CONCEPTS

Egg Hunt

Many people eat eggs laid by chickens.
Some chickens lay colorful eggs.

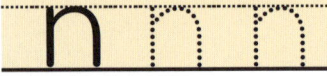

A Let's get cracking!

Draw a line from each egg to the nest where it belongs.

Picky Eaters

Animals have favorite foods, just like you!

Draw a line from the animal to the type of food it is eating.

Cool Tools

Farmers need tools to help them do their work. Tools can help with jobs like digging and planting. Do you have tools at home?

Farmer's Helpers

Where are the farmer's tools? Circle the tools that belong on the farm.

LETTERS **WRITING**

O is for Overalls

Overalls are a kind of clothing that some farmers wear to protect them while they are working.

Trace and then write O and o. What sound does this letter make?

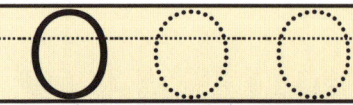

Oooo ... I See It!

The word tool has more than one o.

Draw an X on the pictures that show something that starts with O.

Horses can be very helpful to farmers because they can pull heavy tools.

overalls

orange

shovel

flower

oatmeal

book

Pigpen Playtime!

Why are pigs often covered in mud? Pigs roll in mud to keep cool! Mud also helps protect pigs from getting a sunburn.

LETTERS **WRITING**

P is for Pig

Trace and then write **P** and **p**. What sound does this letter make?

P P P

p p p

MATH

Pig Pals

How many pigs can you find? Circle the answer.

5   6   7

A Standout Pig

Which pig is different? Circle it.
Then color the pigs.

Q What do you call the story "The Three Little Pigs"?

A A pig tale!

Make a Splash

Some farms have ponds. Ducks often live near ponds! Ducks have webbed feet that help them swim.

LETTERS | **WRITING**

Q is for Quack!

Ducks make the sound quack. Now you try making the sound!

Trace and then write Q and q. What sound does this letter make?

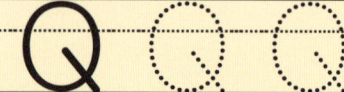

Ducks sometimes sleep with one eye open to look out for danger.

Duck After Duck

Which pond has more ducks? Count the ducks in each pond. Circle the answers.

5   6   7

8   9   10

Cock-a-doodle-doo!

A rooster is a male chicken. A hen is a female chicken. Roosters make loud calls in the early morning!

hen
rooster

LETTERS **WRITING**

R is for Rooster

Trace and then write R and r.
What sound does this letter make?

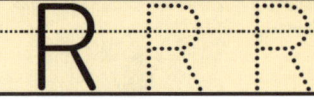

EARLY CONCEPTS **MATH**

Terrific Triangles

The rooster scratched a triangle in the barnyard.

Trace the triangle. Then draw 4 more in the boxes.

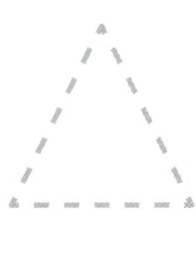

Big Boy!

Draw a rooster that is bigger than the one shown.

The spikes on a rooster's head are called a comb. The comb helps the rooster stay cool.

Super Silos

What's that tall tower on the farm? It's a silo! Farmers can store grain in silos. The grain can be used to feed animals.

Piles of Corn

Can you name one food that is stored in silos? Corn!

Circle the pile of corn kernels that is the largest. Draw an X on the one that is the smallest.

Corn isn't just food! Parts of corn plants can be found in shampoo, paper, and even clothing.

LETTERS **WRITING**

S is for Silo

Trace and then write S and s. What sound does this letter make?

S S S

s s s

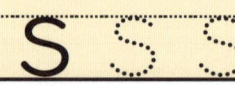

Silo Sight Words

Color each silo that has a word that begins with the letter a.

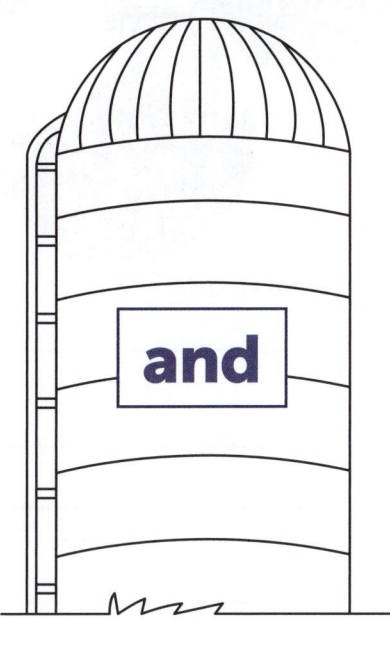

and

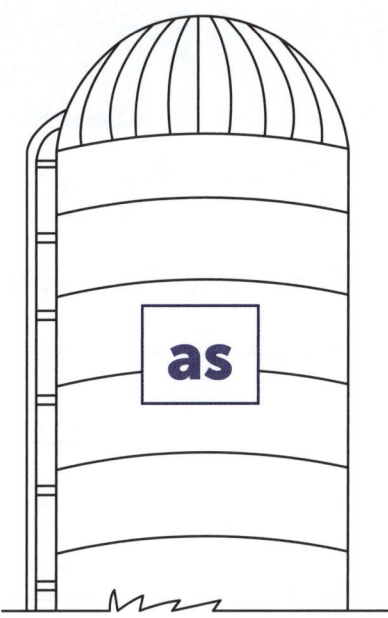

as

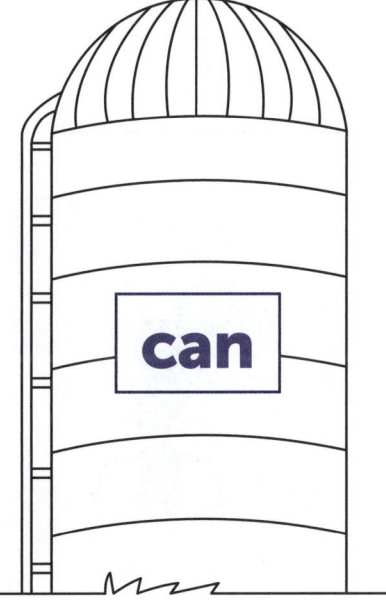

can

is

at

Terrific Tractors

Farmers use tractors to pull big tools! The tractor below is pulling a tiller. A tiller breaks up soil to make planting easier.

LETTERS **WRITING**

T is for Tiller

Trace and then write T and t. What sound does this letter make?

LETTERS

T Time

The farmer is collecting words!

Make an X next to the pictures of words that start with t.

ant

tree

tortoise

tent

butterfly

Collect the Corn

Help the tractor harvest the corn. Follow the letter T to reach the barn.

? Many tractors are painted green and yellow. What colors would you paint your tractor?

So Many Spots

Many cows have spots. The spots come in all shapes and sizes. A cow's spots can even confuse bugs and keep them away!

LETTERS **WRITING**

U is for Useful

Cows are useful for the milk they make.

Trace and then write U and u. What sound does this letter make?

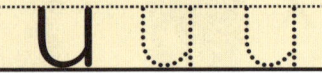

U U U

u u u

MATH

Spot the Spots!

Count each animal's spots. Circle the right numbers.

| 7 | 8 | 2 | 4 | 4 | 6 |

Who Does Not Belong?

All of these animals have spots, but not all of them live on a farm.

Draw a check mark on the animal that does not live on a farm.

Farm Fun

You saw plants and animals on your trip to the farm. What was your favorite thing to see?

EARLY CONCEPTS

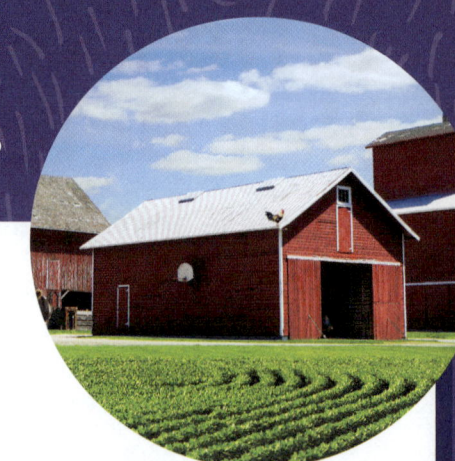

Farm Fresh

Color these vegetables that grow on farms.

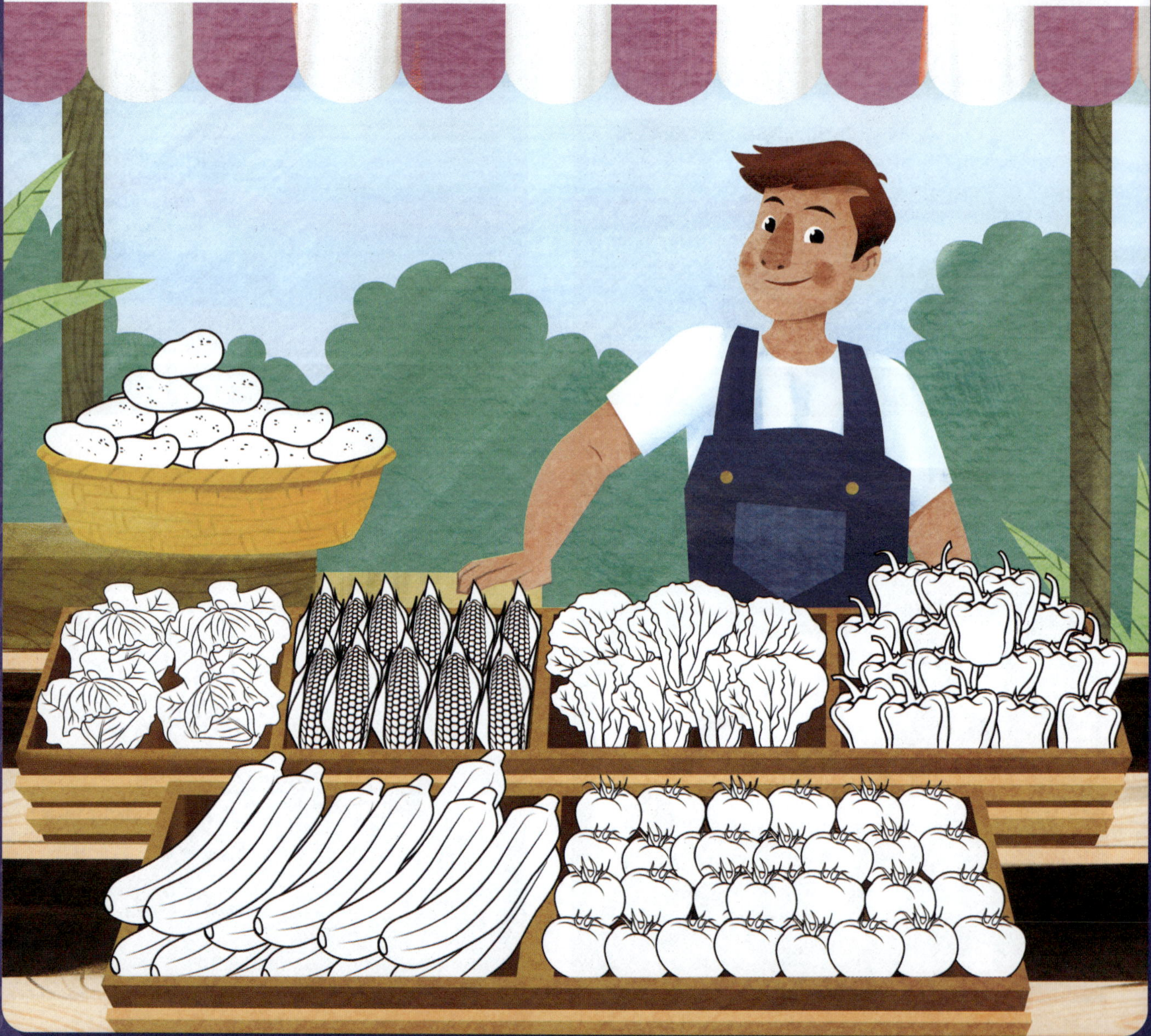

A Farmer's Friend

Connect the dots in the right order from **1** to **10** to finish drawing the farm animal. Then color the picture.

CHAPTER 3

Wonderful Weather

Take a peek outside. Is it windy, rainy, sunny, cloudy, or snowy? The weather can be different every day, and it changes really fast! In this chapter, you'll learn some amazing facts about the weather and how it can affect what you do each day.

Weather can be wild! During big storms, balls of ice called hail sometimes fall from the sky. Hail can be bigger than a baseball!

A Foggy Day

Clouds are made of tiny drops of water. They can float up high or near the ground. A cloud floating near the ground is called fog!

LETTERS **WRITING**

V is for Vapor

When drops of water in the air turn into a gas, it is called water vapor. Water vapor is invisible.

Trace and then write V and v. What sound does this letter make?

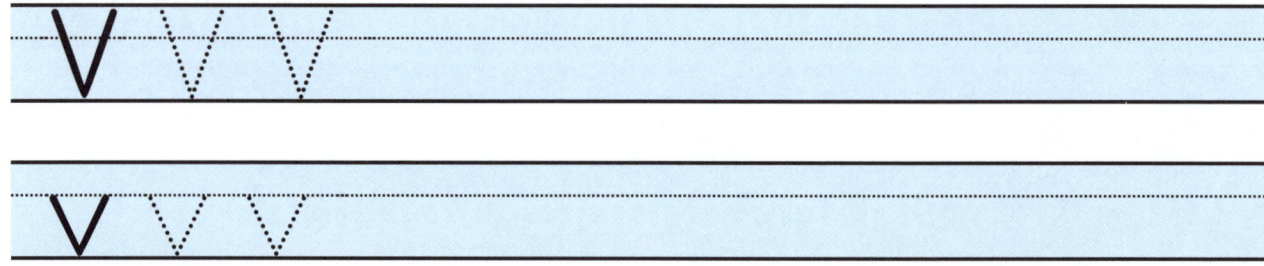

LETTERS

What Starts With V?

Which words start with v? Put a △ around the things that start with the letter v.

Lost in the Fog

It's hard to see in the fog!

Follow the maze to help the fawn find the mother deer.

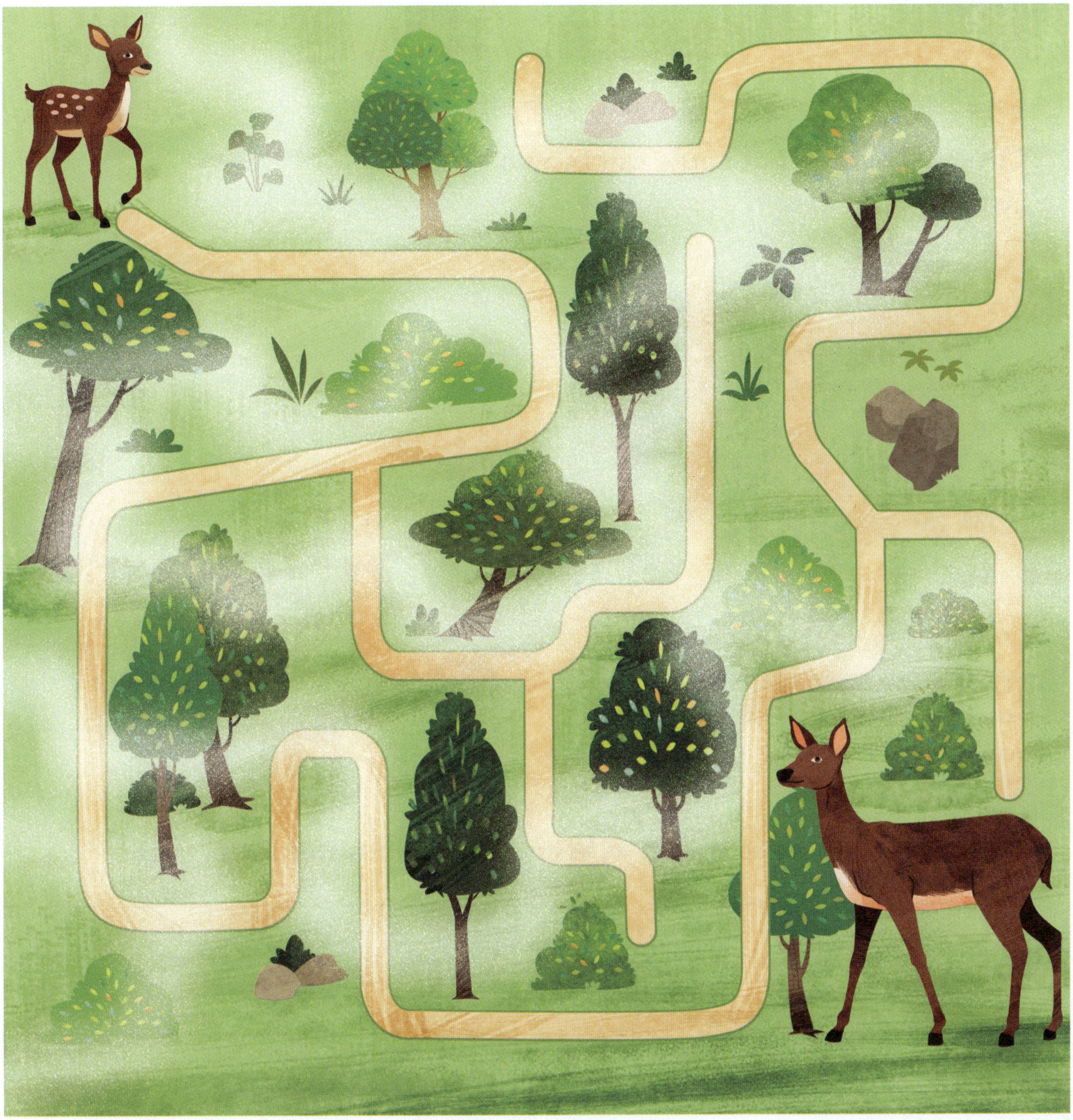

? Do you think fog feels wet or dry? Why?

Wild Wind

Wind is moving air. Wind can blow gently. It can also blow very hard! You can't see wind, but you can see when it moves things.

Blow, Breeze, Blow!

Breeze is another word for wind. It is a breezy day!

Circle the items that could get blown away by a breeze.

LETTERS   WRITING

W is for Wind

Trace and then write W and w. What sound does this letter make?

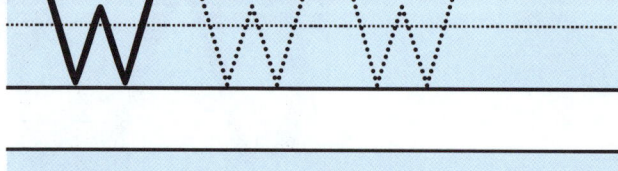

W w w

W w w

Counting Clouds

The wind moves clouds across the sky.

The girl is watching them move.

Count the number of clouds she can see.
Circle the number.

4   5   6

Extreme Weather

Some weather is extreme! This means it's especially strong and can be dangerous. Have you seen any extreme weather where you live?

LETTERS | **WRITING**

X is in Extreme

X is one of the letters in extreme.

Trace and then write X and x. What sound does this letter make?

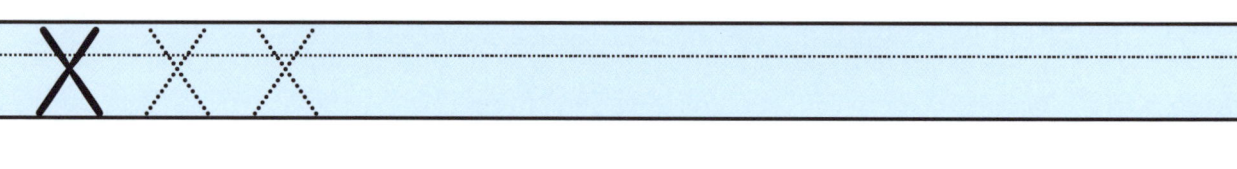

EARLY CONCEPTS

Which Is Wilder?

A hurricane is one kind of extreme weather. It is a storm with rain and strong wind.

Circle the picture that shows very strong wind.

Tornado Count

A tornado is another kind of extreme weather. It is a column of wind that spins very quickly.

Count groups of 10. How many groups of 10 tornadoes do you see? Write the number.

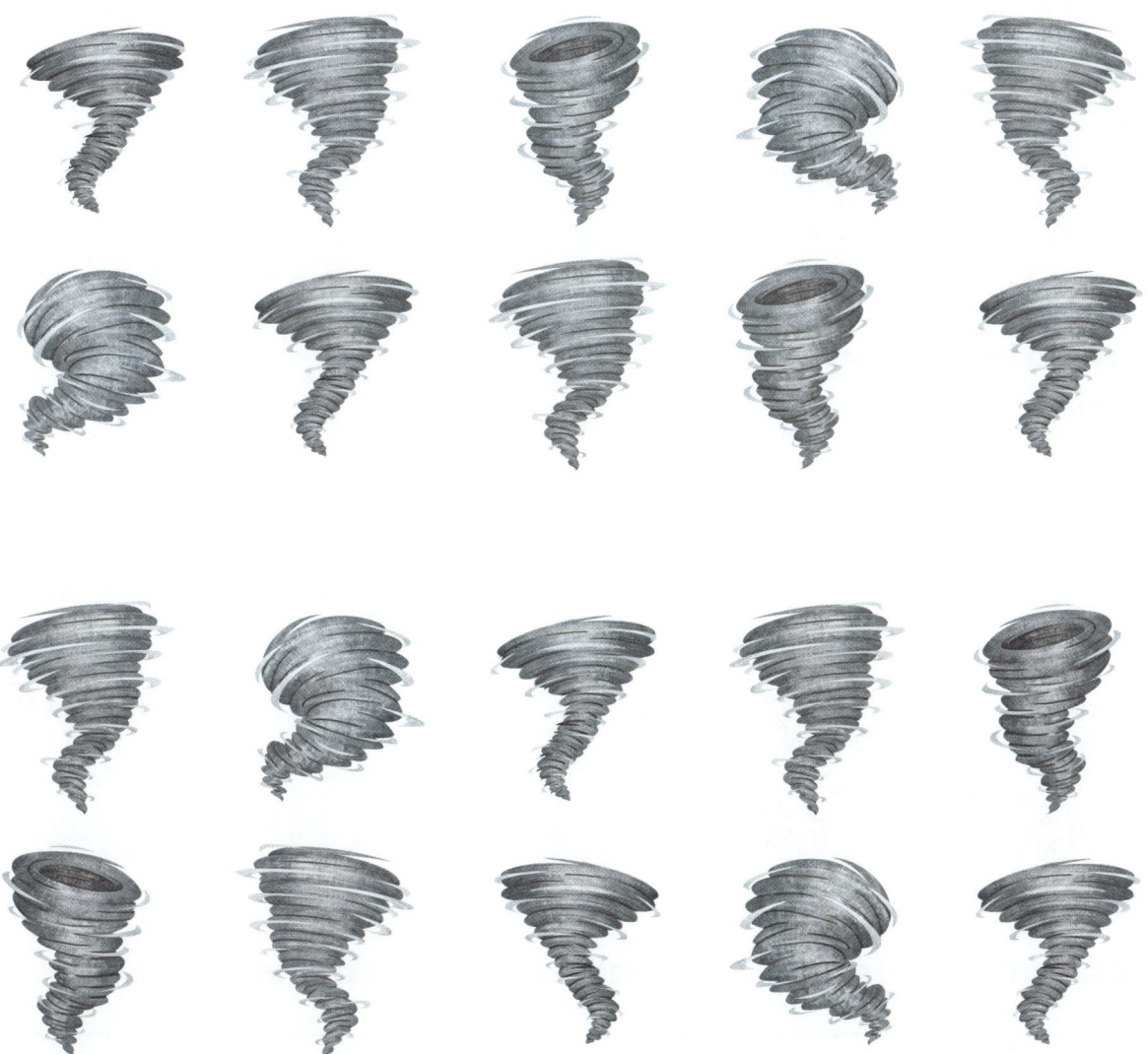

_____ groups of 10 tornadoes makes 20 tornadoes.

A Year of Weather

In many places on Earth, weather changes with the seasons. Summer is often warm and sunny. In winter it can be much colder!

MATH

Summer Sun

The sun is so bright in the summer! Light from the sun goes out in all directions.

Draw 10 lines, or rays, on the sun.

LETTERS **WRITING**

Y is for Year

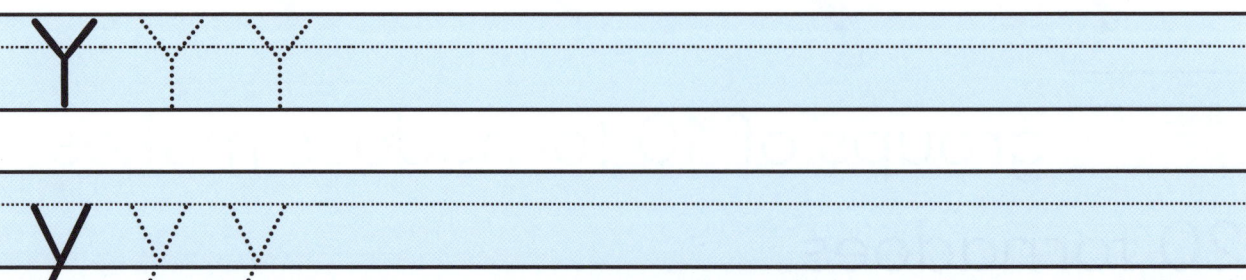

Weather is different every day of the year.

Trace and then write Y and y. What sound does this letter make?

Y Y Y

y y y

What to Wear?

We wear different clothes in different weather.

Draw lines to match the clothes with the weather.

Ba-Boom!

Lightning is a burst of electricity that can look like a zigzag in the sky! Thunder is the booming sound of lightning.

LETTERS **WRITING**

Z is for Zigzag

Trace and then write **Z** and **z**. What sound does this letter make?

Z Z Z Z

z z z z

MATH **WRITING**

Count the Bolts

Count the number of lightning bolts in the picture. Write the number on the line.

There are _____ lightning bolts.

A lightning bolt is hotter than the sun!

Lightning Flash

Trace the lightning bolts from the clouds to the ground.

Follow the Rainbow

When sunlight shines through drops of rain, you may see a rainbow. Rainbows show the colors of light.

READING **WRITING**

Trace and Write "and"

Sun **and** rain make a rainbow.

Trace the word and. Then write and on the line.

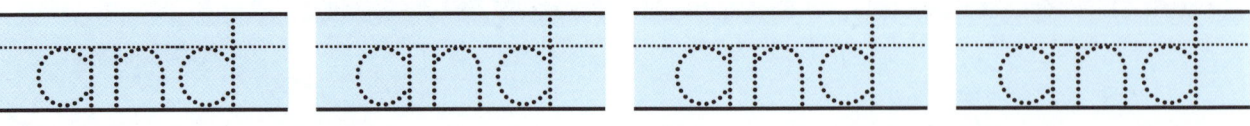

Color Your Own

The colors of a rainbow are always in the same order.

Color in the rest of the rainbow. Use the number key to find the right colors.

Q What kind of bow can't be tied?

Number key

1 - red   2 - orange   3 - green   4 - blue   5 - violet

1
2
3
4
5

A   A rainbow!

Drip, Drop!

What makes it rain? Drops of water in the clouds get big and heavy. They begin to fall to the ground. It's raining!

LETTERS **WRITING**

Missing Letters

Oh, no! The rain washed away some letters!

Look at the photos. What is the beginning sound of the thing in each picture? Write the missing beginning sound for each word. Choose from the letters in the box.

d   c   r

____loud

____ain

____rop

MATH

Find the 4s

Sometimes water from the rain forms a puddle.

Circle the number 4s that are in this puddle.

EARLY CONCEPTS

What Do We Need Today?

Circle the things we use when it's raining. Draw an X on the ones we don't use on a rainy day.

Falling Snowflakes

Snow may fall when it is cold outside. Snowflakes are tiny pieces of ice. All snowflakes have six points. Every snowflake is different!

MATH

6 Points

Can you find the shape with 6 points? Color it.

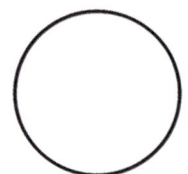  

EARLY CONCEPTS

Snowflake Patterns

Which snowflake comes next in each pattern? Circle it.

      |

      |

Snowflakes on My Head!

It's starting to snow! Connect the dots in the right order from 1 to 10. See the shape of the snowflake falling from the sky.

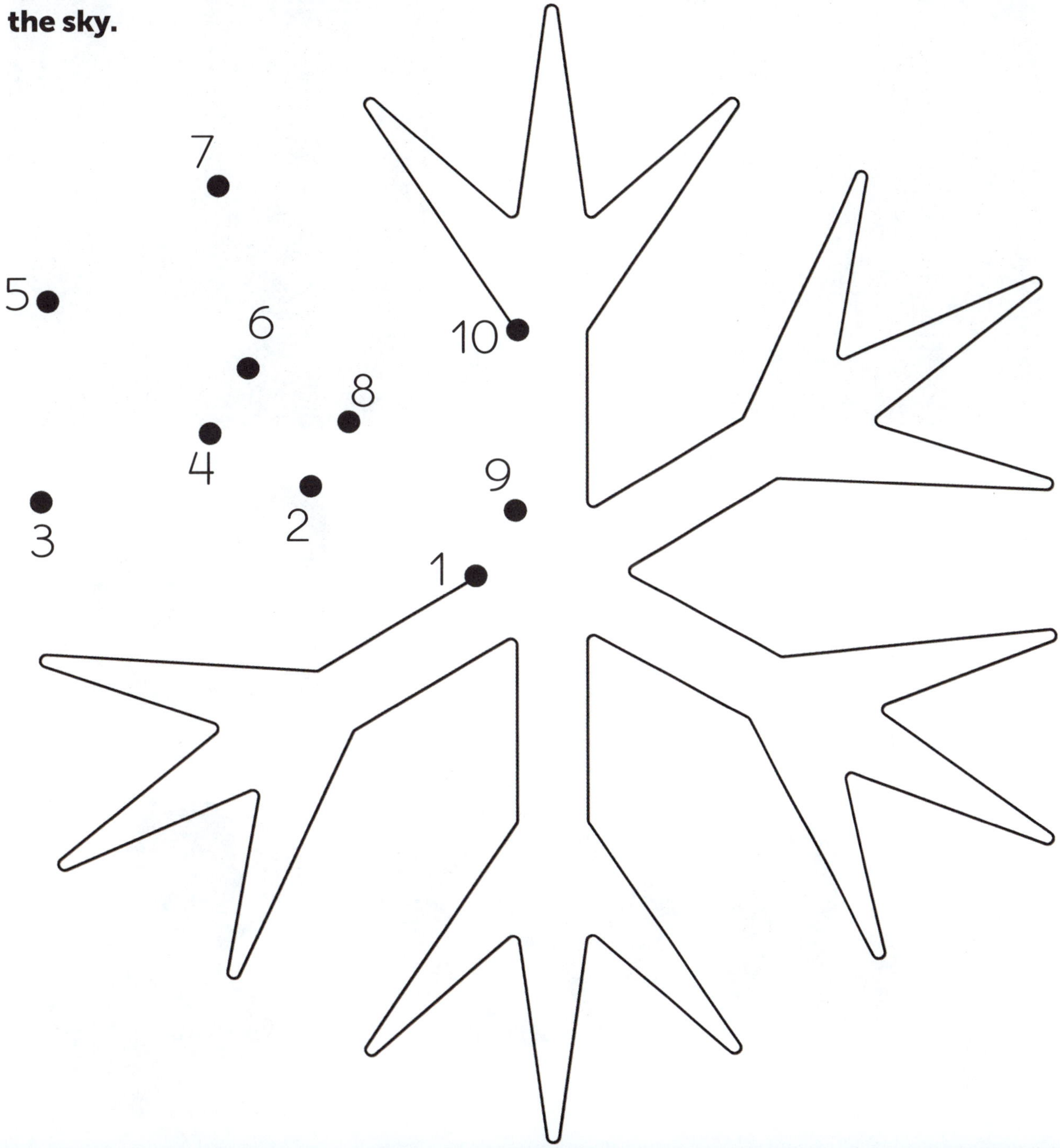

7

5

6

8

10

4

3

2

9

1

A Sunny Day

Some days are sunny and bright. Sunshine warms Earth and helps plants grow. There's a lot we can do outside on a sunny day!

Playtime

Circle the activities that are usually done outside on sunny days.

A Walk Through the Garden

Walk through the garden on a sunny day.

Follow the maze to reach the picnic table.

It takes eight minutes and 20 seconds for light to travel from the sun to Earth.

75

Up in the Clouds

Clouds have different shapes. Some are puffy and fluffy. Some are thin and wavy.

MATH

Cloud Counter

The clouds show the numbers from **10** to **16**. But some numbers blew away! Fill in the missing numbers.

10   11   _____

13   _____   _____   16

Colorful Clouds

What letter does the word is start with? Find the clouds that have a word that starts with the same letter. Color them.

in

on

if

up

it

What's the Weather?

A weather forecast tells you what the weather might be like in the future. It tells you if it will be sunny, rainy, snowy, warm, or cold.

EARLY CONCEPTS

Be Prepared!

A weather forecast helps you prepare for your day.

The weather forecast says it will be rainy. Draw what you will wear.

? Why do you think people want to know the weather before they start their day?

Draw the Forecast

Read each weather forecast. Draw a picture to show the weather that day.

Day	Forecast	Picture
Monday	Sunny	
Tuesday	Cloudy	
Wednesday	Rainy	
Thursday	Snowy	
Friday	Windy	

Weather on the Go

Here's a final fact about the weather: It's always changing! Weather can change during a single day or even a single hour! Wherever you go, there will always be some kind of weather.

A Curious Sky

What kind of weather did you explore in this chapter that you'd like to know more about? Draw it!

A Rainy Day Pal

It's starting to rain!

What do you need to take with you to stay dry? Connect the dots in the right order from A to Z to find out.

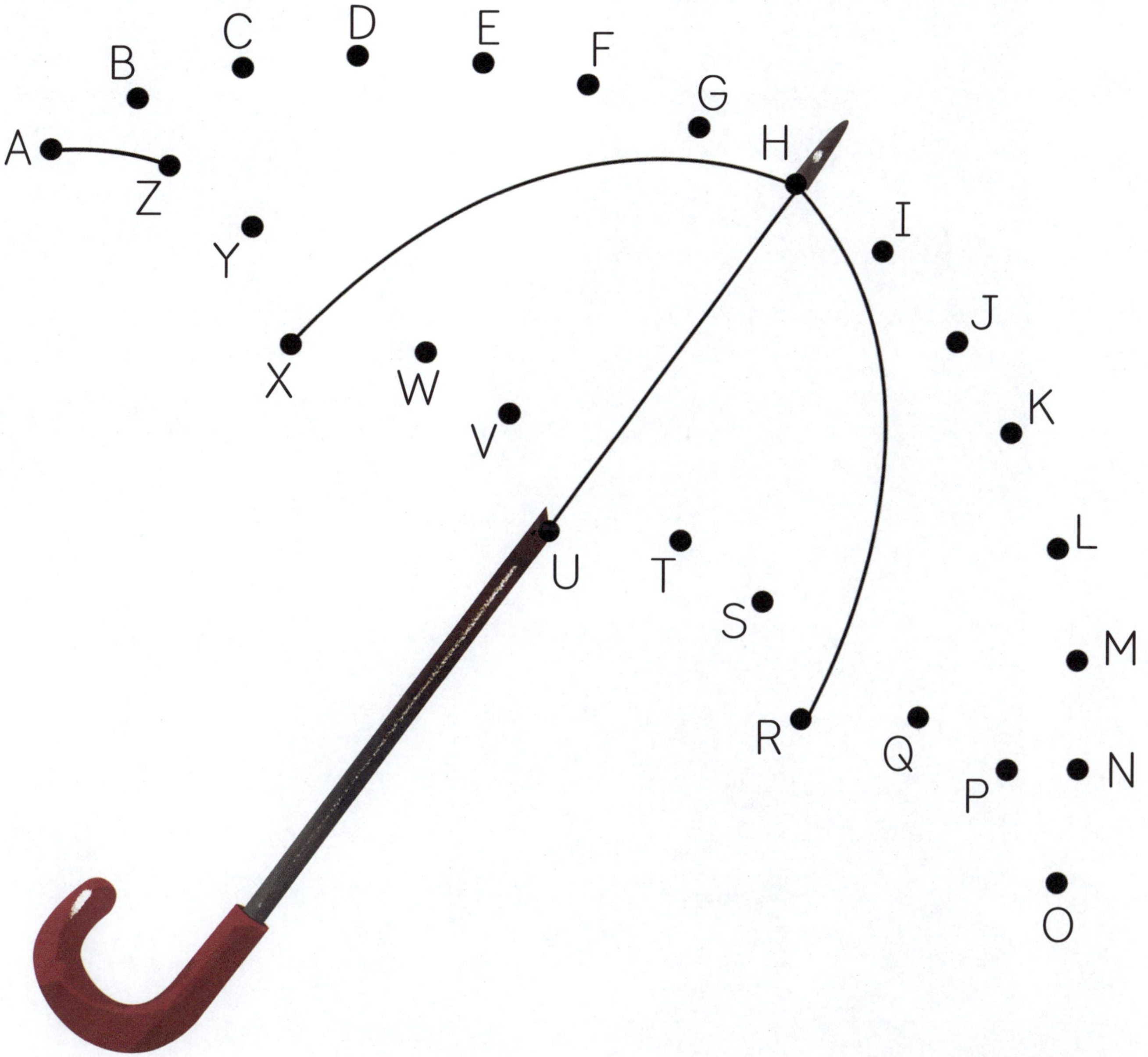

B
C
D
E
F
A
Z
G
H
Y
I
X
J
W
V
K
L
U
T
S
M
R
Q
N
P
O

CHAPTER 4

Space Adventure

Look up into the night sky. There's so much out there! In this chapter, you'll look at the stars, moons, and planets. As you read, imagine what it might be like to be a space explorer!

SATURN

Some planets, like Saturn, are made of gas instead of rock.

Blast Off!

This rocket is headed to space! Some rockets carry astronauts. Other rockets carry tools that help us study space.

EARLY CONCEPTS **MATH**

Rocket Shapes

Color the shapes that make up the rocket. Use the colors shown here for each shape.

What do you think might be inside this rocket?

MATH WRITING

Countdown to Liftoff

Count backward from 10 to 1 as the rocket gets ready to go into space. Trace the numbers.

10
9
8
7
6
5
4
3
2
1
We have liftoff!

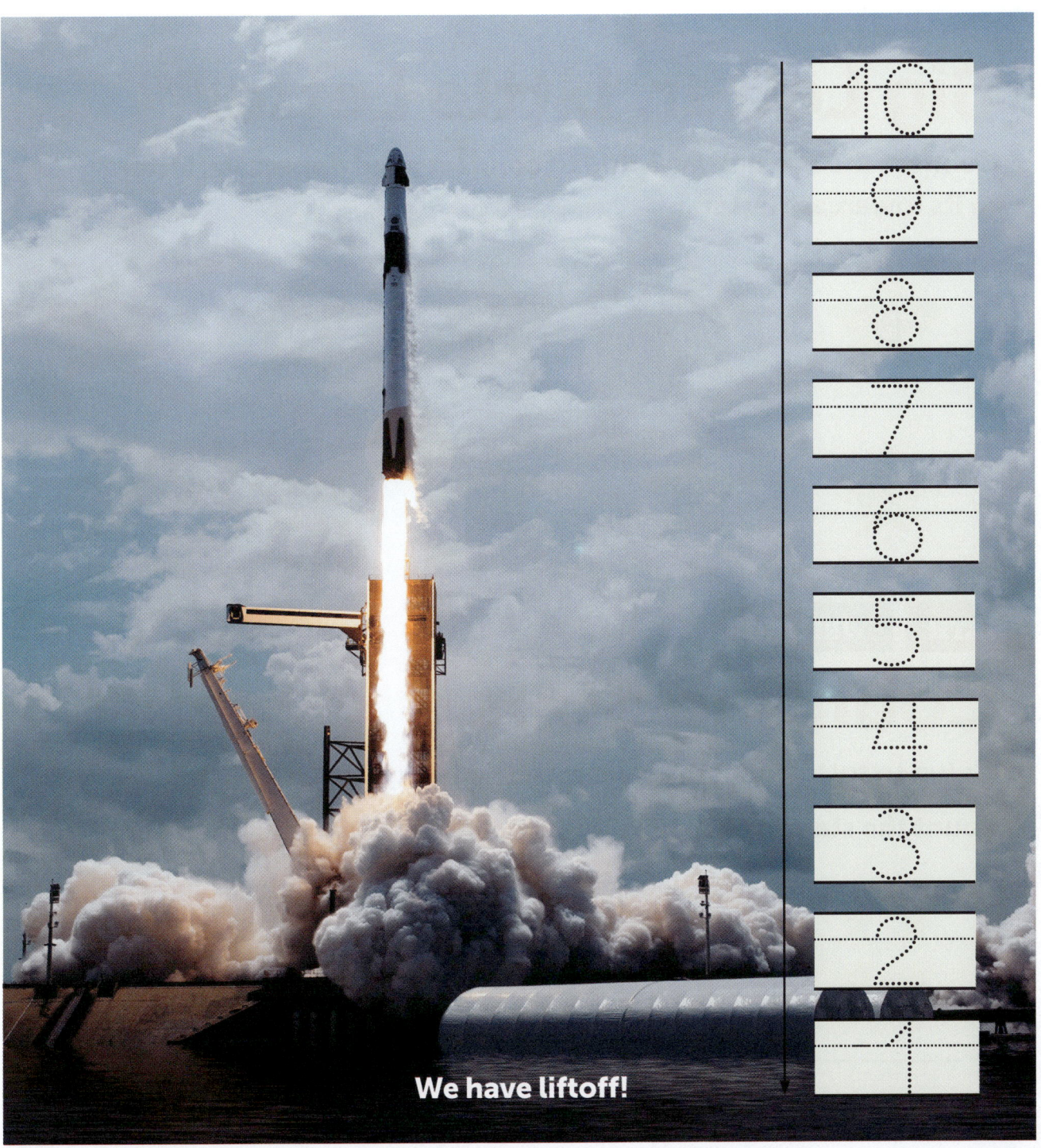

Super Stars

From Earth, most stars look like tiny lights in the sky. But stars are huge! They are superhot balls of gas that make light.

LETTERS

Big Letter, Little Letter

Connect the stars! Draw a line to connect each uppercase letter to its lowercase letter.

MATH   **WRITING**

Counting Stars

It's fun to try to count the stars in the night sky.

Count the stars in each box. Write the number of stars on the line.

EARLY CONCEPTS

Making Pegasus

Constellations are groups of stars. People see all kinds of pictures in them.

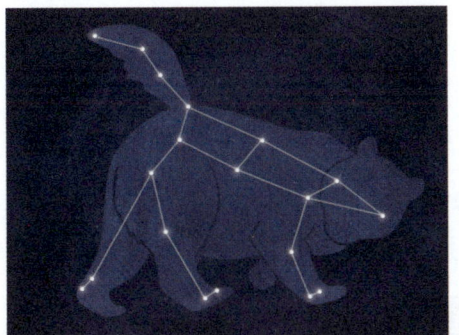

Ursa Major (Great Bear)

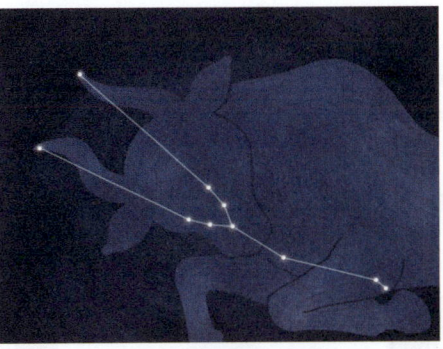

Taurus (Bull)

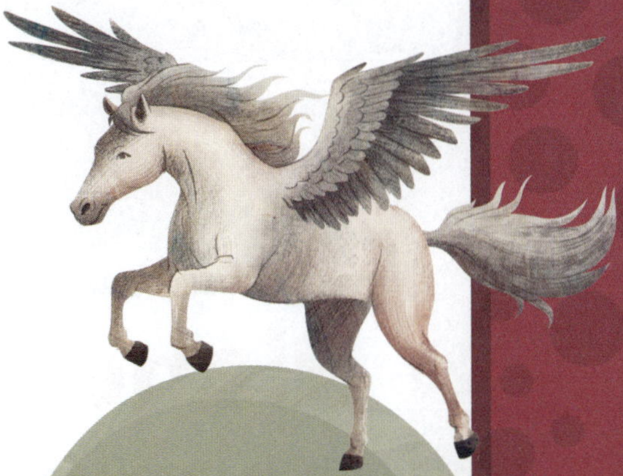

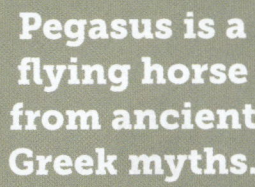

Pegasus is a flying horse from ancient Greek myths.

Trace the lines to complete the Pegasus constellation.

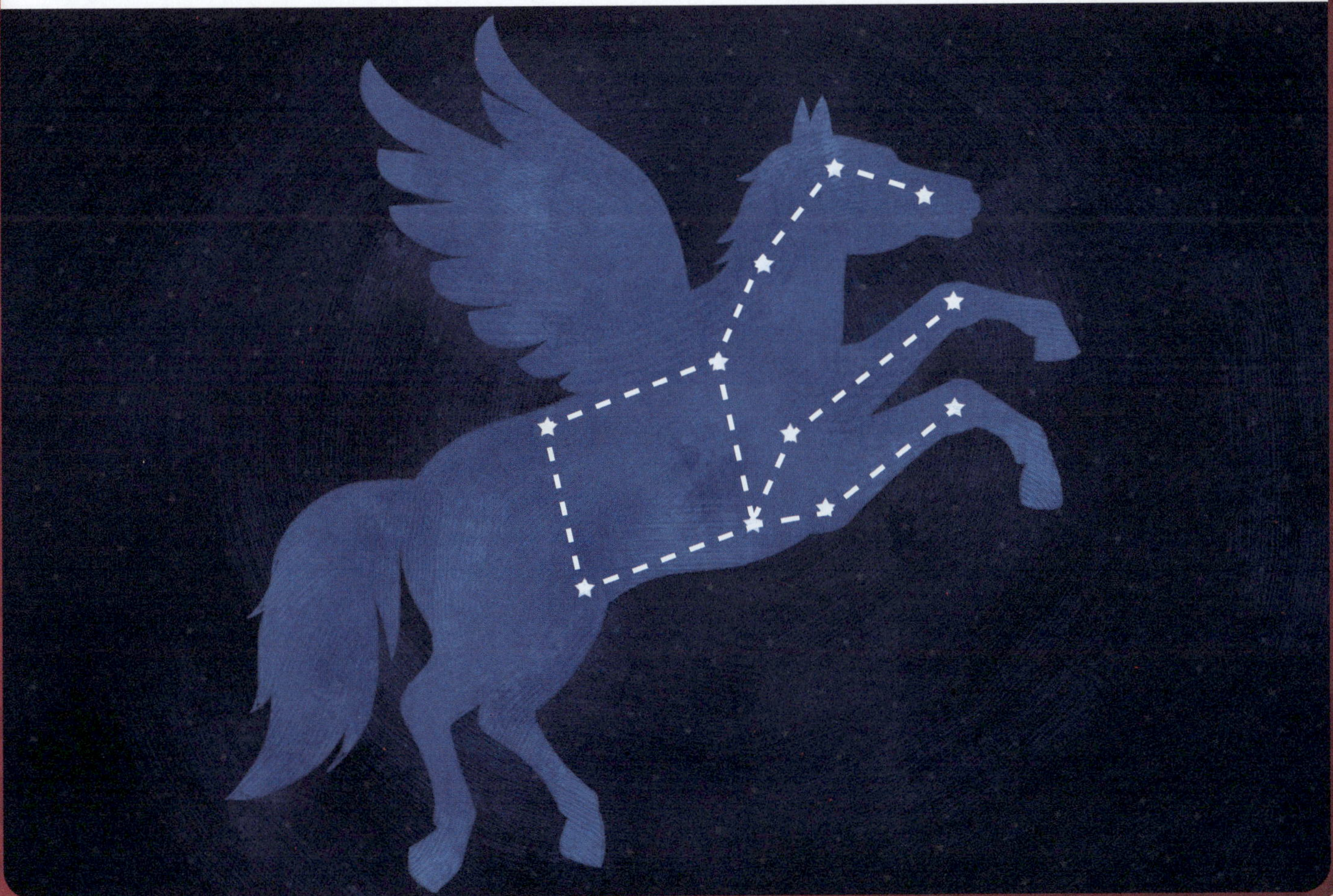

Eight Great Planets

The eight planets in our solar system all move around the sun.
Do you know which planet is closest to the sun? Mercury!

Planet Patterns

Circle the planet that comes next in each pattern.

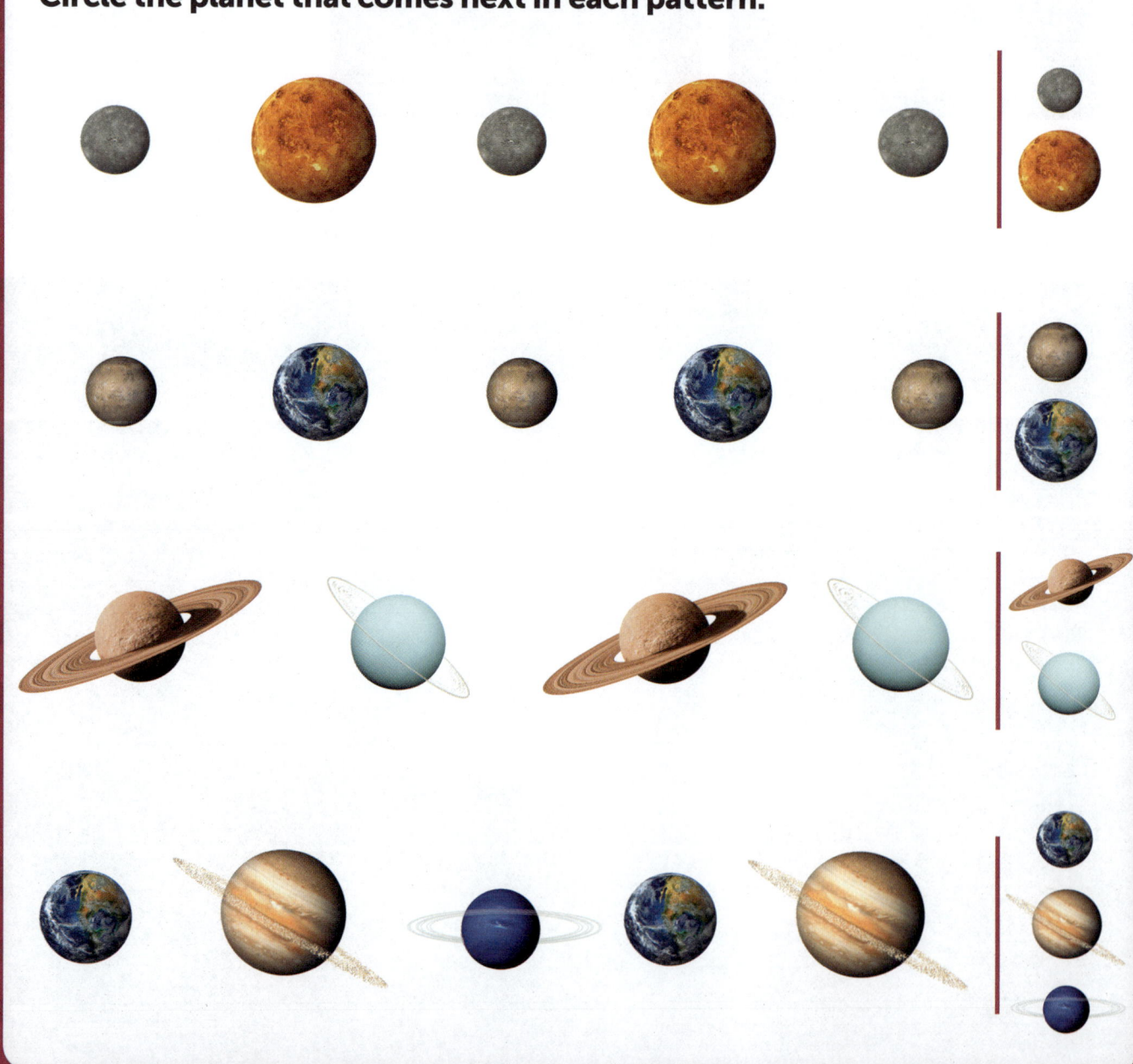

Q How can you have a party in space?

Name Them All!

These are all the planets in our solar system in order, from closest to the sun to farthest away.

Trace the first letter of each planet. What sound does that letter make? Then circle the planets that have rings around them.

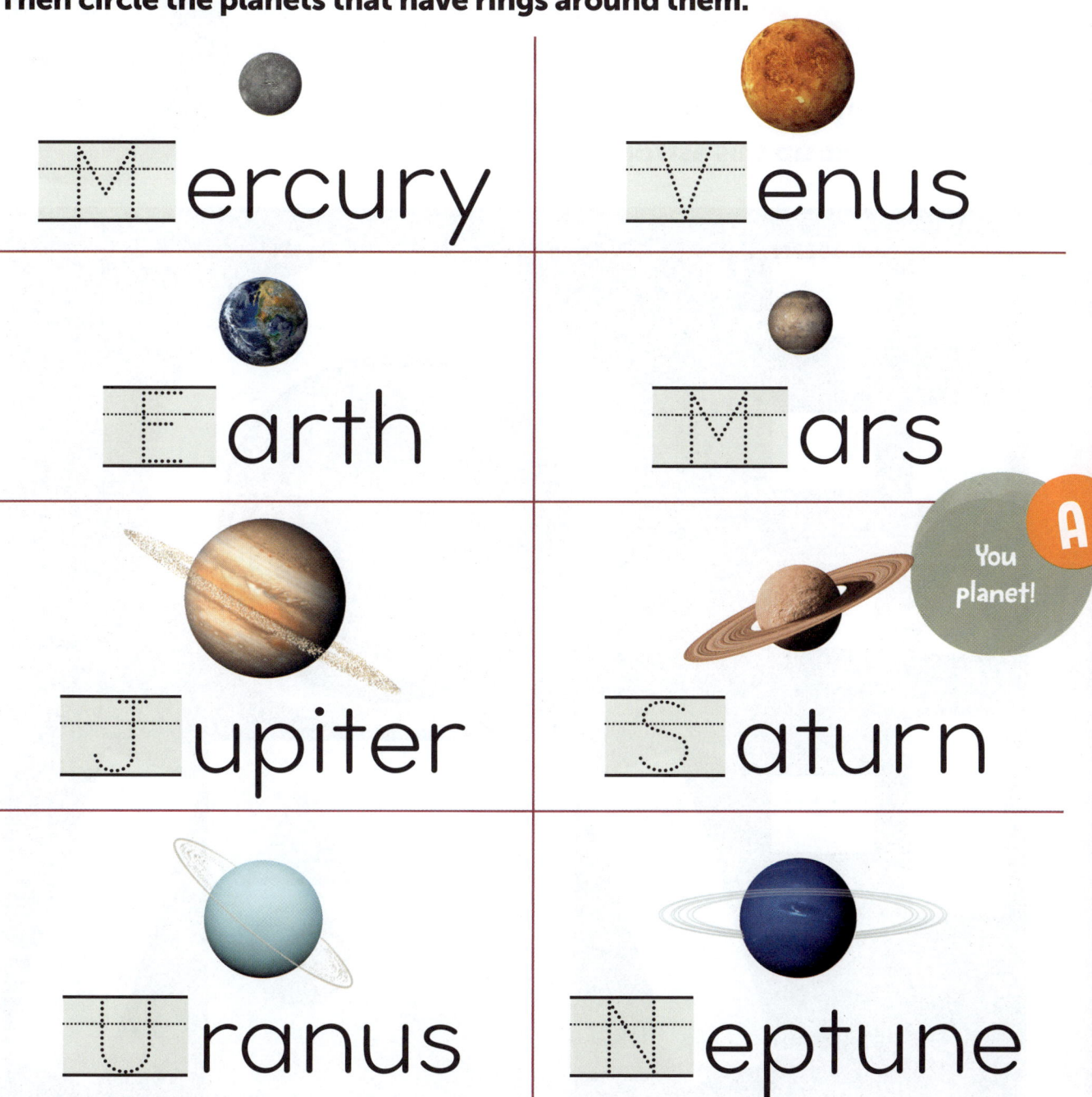

Mercury

Venus

Earth

Mars

Jupiter

Saturn

You planet!

A

Uranus

Neptune

Awesome Astronauts

Astronauts are people who go to space to study and explore.
Outside their spacecraft, they need special suits for protection.

MATH   **WRITING**

Space Suit Shapes

Count how many circles, rectangles, squares, and triangles make up this astronaut's space suit.

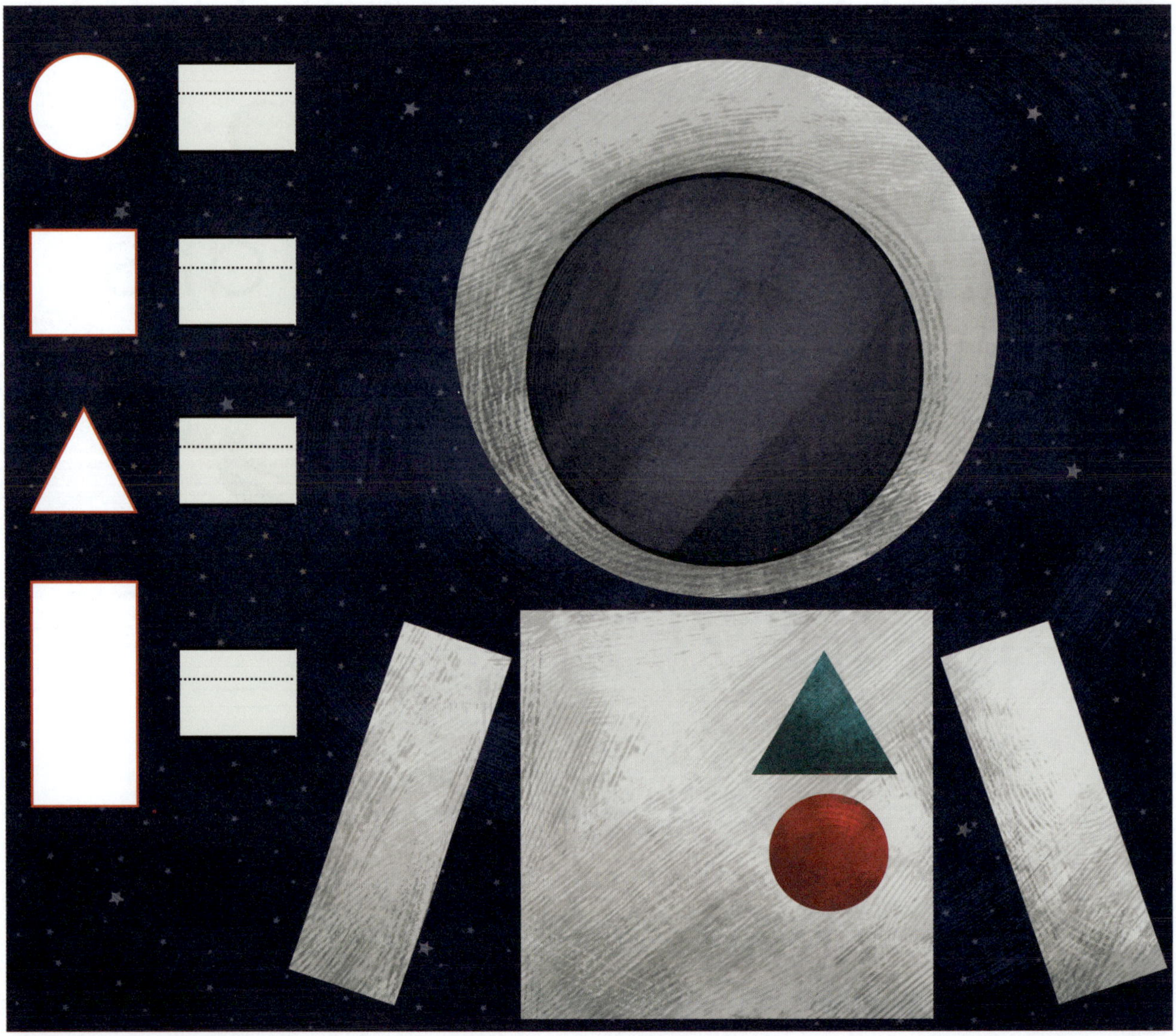

Taking a Moonwalk

This astronaut is walking on the moon!

Help her find her way by writing the letters of the alphabet in order from A to J along the path.

Astronauts first went to the moon in 1969. Some of them even walked on the moon's surface.

The Space Station

The International Space Station is a science lab in space! It orbits, or circles, around Earth. Astronauts live there for many months.

MATH | **WRITING**

Who's Coming on Board?

Draw a line connecting each astronaut to the space station. Then count how many lines you drew and write the number below.

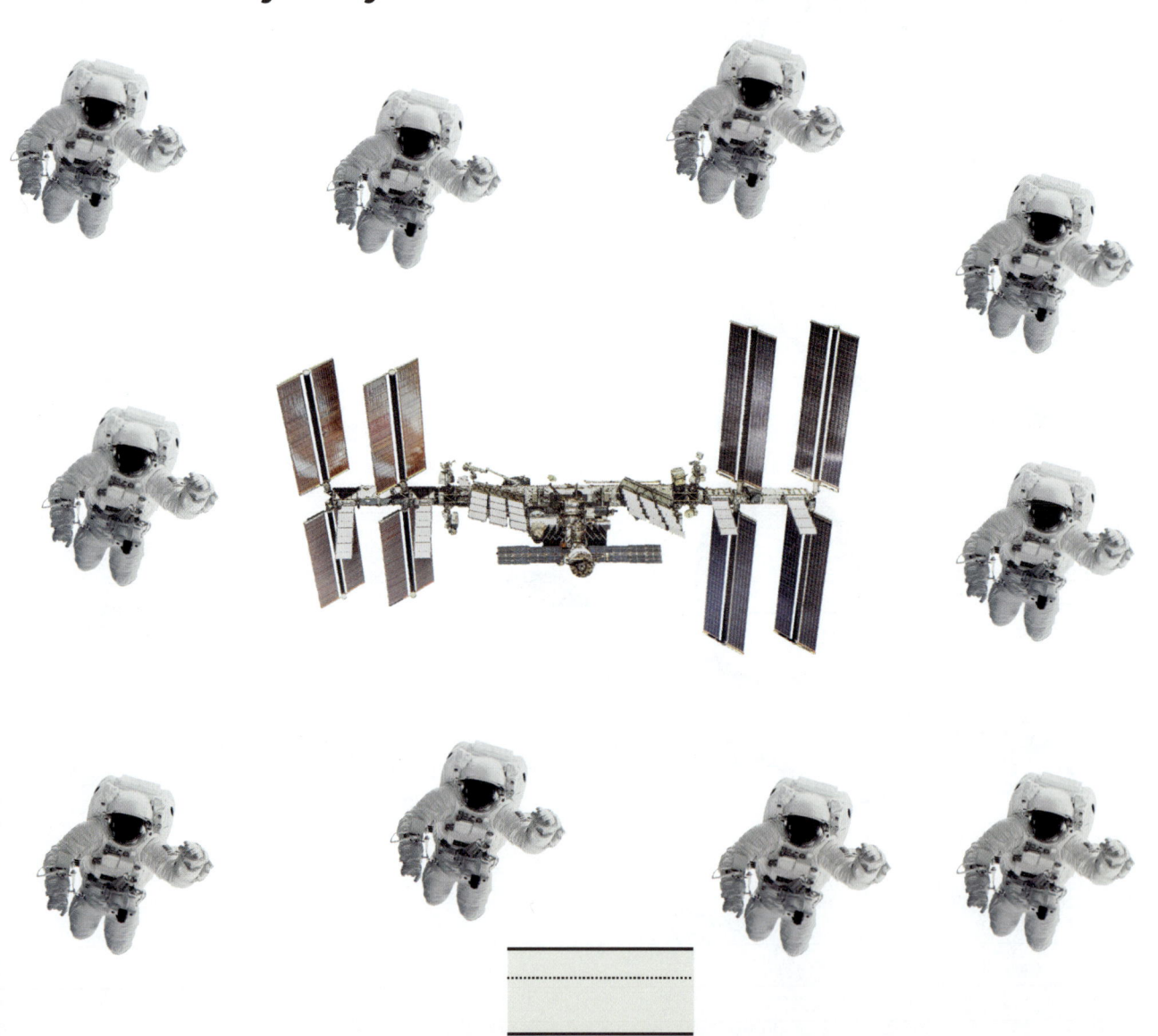

Exploring the Station

Astronauts float in the space station because there is very little gravity in space. Gravity is a force that keeps us on the ground.

Help the astronaut float through the space station maze!

? What do you think astronauts do on board the International Space Station?

Mighty Moons

Q Why did the moon have a bellyache?

A moon is a large object that circles around a planet. Earth has one moon. Jupiter has more than 90!

LETTERS

Moon Words

Draw an **X** in the box if the word has the same starting sound as the word **moon**.

MATH   **WRITING**

Many Moons

The picture shows **7** moons of Jupiter.

Draw **3** more. How many are there now? Write the number on the line.

There is no wind on Earth's moon. A footprint on the moon will take a very long time to disappear!

Counting Craters

A crater is a large hole in the ground.

Count the craters on the moon. Write the number.

A It was full!

Exploring Mars

Humans have not yet traveled to Mars. We have sent robots called rovers to study the planet. They take pictures and videos.

EARLY CONCEPTS **MATH**

Your Own Rover

Draw your own space rover. Include squares, circles, and rectangles in your drawing.

EARLY CONCEPTS

Roving Around

Help the rover take pictures of Mars!

Find a path for the rover to follow through the maze.

END

Terrific Telescopes

A telescope makes faraway objects seem closer. You can use a telescope to see objects in space more clearly.

WRITING

Words in the Stars

Trace the words the telescope found in space.

can

pan

man

ran

fan

Star Search

Count the stars each telescope sees.
Which view shows more stars? Circle it!

MATH   WRITING

Telescope Counting

How many telescopes do you see below? Draw 4 more.
How many do you have now? Write the total number.

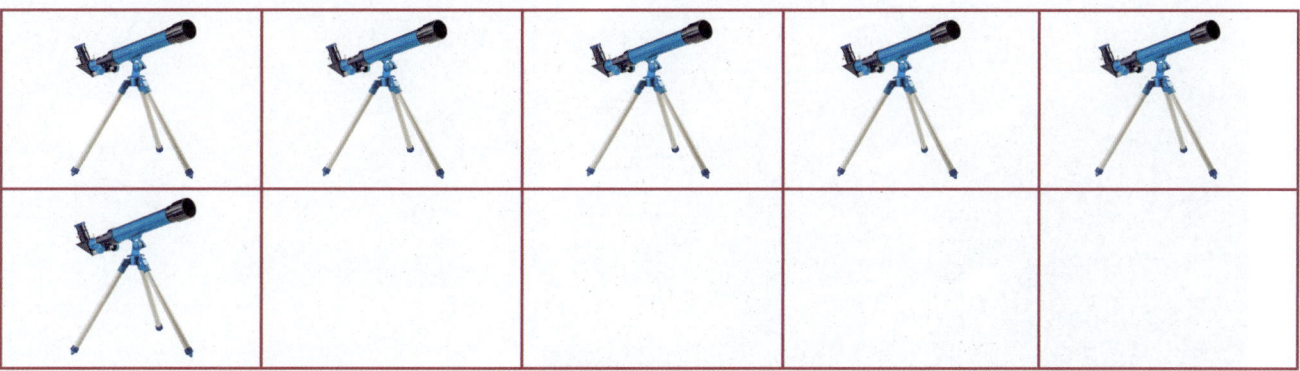

Cool Comets

Comets are chunks of dust, rock, and ice. They move around the sun. They are famous for their long tails made of gas and dust.

On the Lookout

What's that in the sky? Trace the words to complete the sentence.

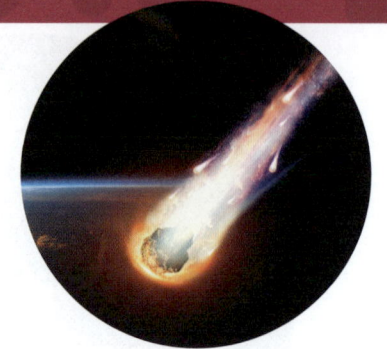

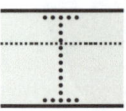 see 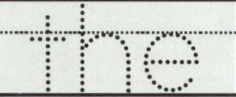 big comet.

Counting Comets

Count the comets. Write the number on the line.

Comet Sort

Can you find the comets? Draw an **X** next to each comet. What other space objects do you see?

Comets are sometimes called dirty snowballs.

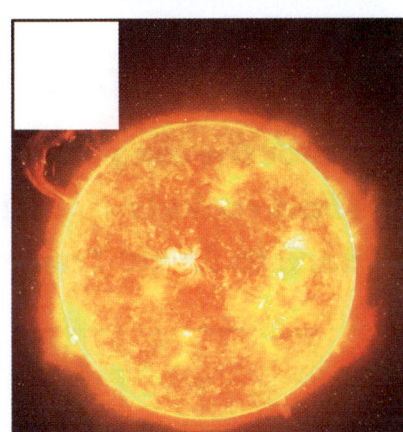

Back to Earth

When spacecraft return to Earth, some land like a plane. Some land in the ocean. Others land upright, standing tall!

EARLY CONCEPTS　**READING**　**WRITING**

Rockets Return

Color the long rockets **blue**. Color the short rockets **red**. Where are they going? Back to Earth! Trace the word **Earth**.

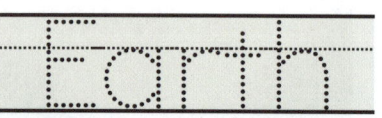

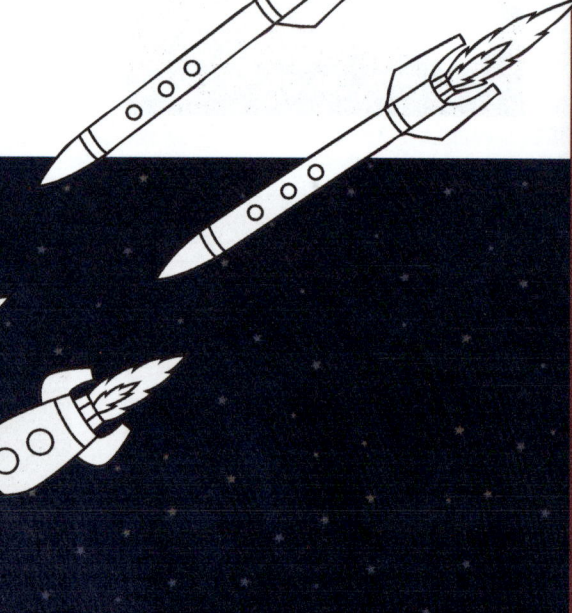

Safe Landing

The spacecraft is back home!

Fill in the missing lowercase letters in order from a to z.

Blast Off into Space

Now that you have learned about space, is it someplace you'd like to visit? Imagine taking off into space! Where would you like to go first?

Astronaut Alan Shepard hit golf balls on the moon. One ball landed in a moon crater!

My Moon Landing

Draw your face on the astronaut and then color the rest of the picture. Write your name on the flag!

The word "astronaut" means "star sailor."

CHAPTER 5

Most of Earth's water is found in the oceans.

Water All Around

What comes in tiny drops or huge waves? Water! Plants and animals both need it to survive, and lots of creatures spend their whole lives underwater. In this chapter, get ready to dive deep into the world of water!

All Kinds of Water

We see water in lakes, oceans, and rivers. It falls from the sky as rain. Ice is water that is frozen. Icebergs are made of ice.

EARLY CONCEPTS

Do You See Water?

Look at these places around the world. Draw a check mark next to each place that shows water.

?
What are two kinds of water you can see in this picture?

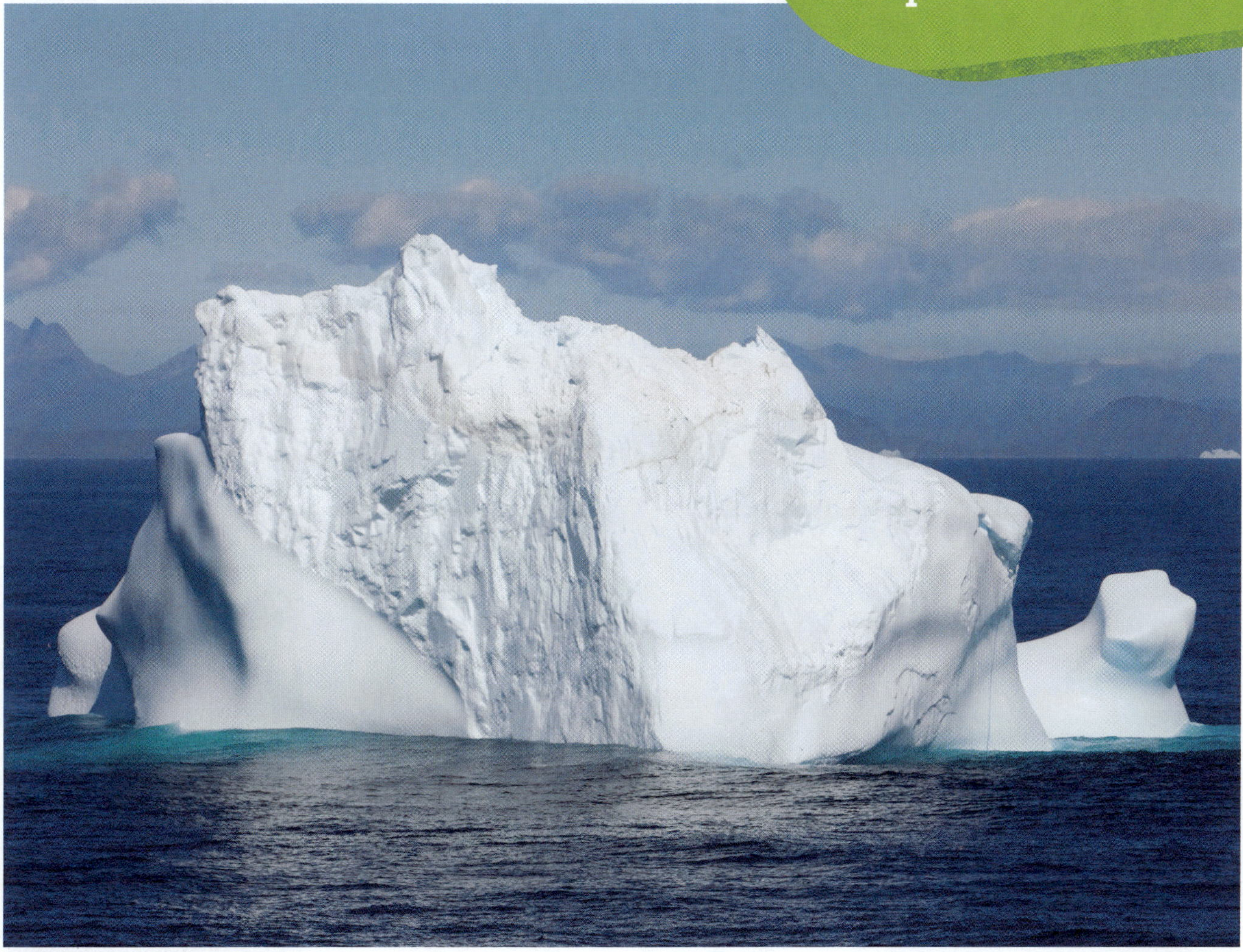

LETTERS

Match the Letters

Draw a line to match each uppercase letter with its lowercase letter.

W	A	T	E	R
t	r	w	a	e

Watery Homes

Some animals must live in water to survive. Other animals must live on land. Some animals can live in both places!

Pick the Home

Which animals live in water? Which live on land? Draw a line from each animal to where it lives.

Alligator's Alphabet

The alligator wants to go for a swim.

Help it find the way by writing the letters of the alphabet in the correct order from A to Z on the path to the river.

A Bubbly Breath

How do fish breathe? Fish have body parts called gills. When water flows over the gills, they take in oxygen from the water.

Most fish don't have eyelids, so they can't blink!

gills

EARLY CONCEPTS · **MATH** · **WRITING**

Finish the Pattern

Look at the pattern of fish and numbers. Write what numbers come next in the boxes.

1   2   1   2

Where Can It Breathe?

Which animals can breathe underwater? Circle them.

Playing at the Pond

Ponds are home to many animals. Fish, frogs, birds, and bugs may live near or in a pond. If you sit quietly, you might hear them.

MATH　**WRITING**

Dragonflies in Flight

These dragonflies are flying fast over the water!

How many dragonflies do you see? Count them. Write the number.

There are ⬚ dragonflies.

Counting Frogs

Which frogs are on lily pads?
Color the frogs on lily pads. Then count them. Write the number.

One dragonfly can eat hundreds of mosquitoes in a single day.

There are ⬜ frogs sitting on lily pads.

Gone Fishing

Let's go fishing! People fish in oceans, lakes, ponds, and rivers. Sometimes people eat the fish they catch.

LETTERS

Catch the Letters!

Try fishing for letters. Draw a line to connect each uppercase letter to its lowercase letter.

G O   F I S   H

s   g   o

i   h   f

Colorful Fish

Fish come in many shapes and sizes.

Color 5 of the fish you see in the picture.

Wondrous Waterfalls

A waterfall happens when a river or stream flows suddenly over a steep drop. Angel Falls is the tallest waterfall in the world.

LETTERS **WRITING**

Falling Letters

Look! Letters are falling over the waterfall.

Trace the letters. Say them out loud. What sound does each letter make?

How Tall Is It?

Waterfalls can be really tall! A ruler shows us how long or tall something is.

Look at each ruler. Circle the number that shows how tall each thing is.

What Kind of Water?

Some bodies of water are small, like ponds. Some are big, like oceans. Some are even frozen! A glacier is a huge sheet of ice.

EARLY CONCEPTS | **LETTERS** | **WRITING**

Terrific Tracing

Here are some places you find water: a lake, the ocean, a river, and a glacier. What is the beginning sound of each place? Trace the letter at the beginning of each word.

lake

ocean

river

glacier

Can You Tell?

Can you tell different kinds of water apart?
Read each question. Point to the answer.

Ocean water weighs more than fresh water because it has salt in it!

1. Which is a glacier?

2. Which is a river?

READING WRITING

Write "go"

What does water do when it flows? It goes! Trace the word go.

   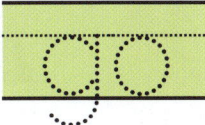 

Now write the word go.

 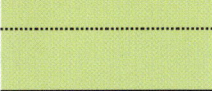 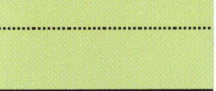  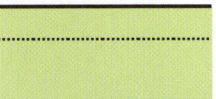

Wave Watching

Have you seen big ocean waves? Many ocean waves are caused by wind. The stronger the winds, the bigger the waves!

MATH **WRITING**

How Many Waves?

Count the waves before they crash on the land! Write the number on the line.

LETTERS **WRITING**

Surf's Up

Fill in the missing letters in order from **T** to **Z** on the surfboards. What comes after **U**?

T U W Z

After the Waves

? Where do you think water in a wave goes after it crashes?

Waves crashed on the shore, leaving seashells behind.

Draw lines to connect the pairs of matching shells.

Sharing Shells

Hermit crabs don't have their own shells. They find empty shells to live in. When a hermit crab grows, it finds a new, bigger shell!

EARLY CONCEPTS

Perfect Patterns

The hermit crab is busy finding new shells.

Circle the picture that continues each pattern.

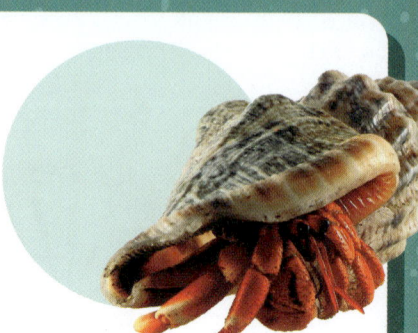

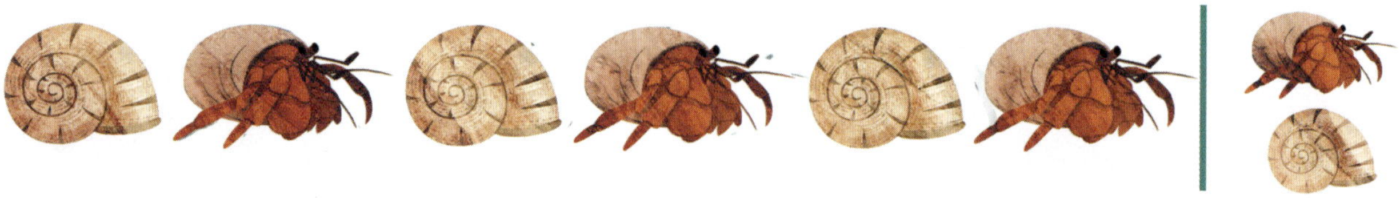

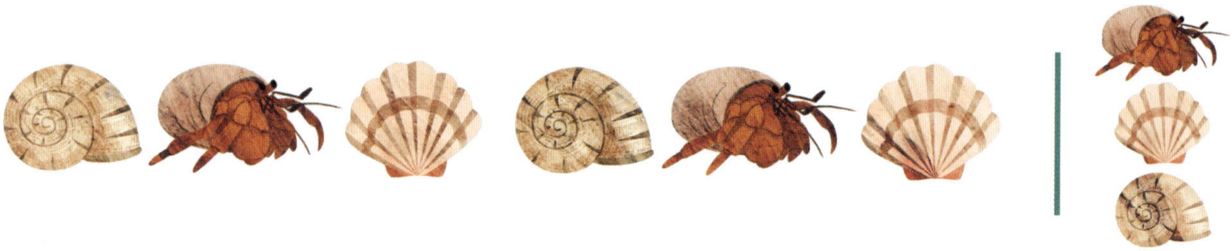

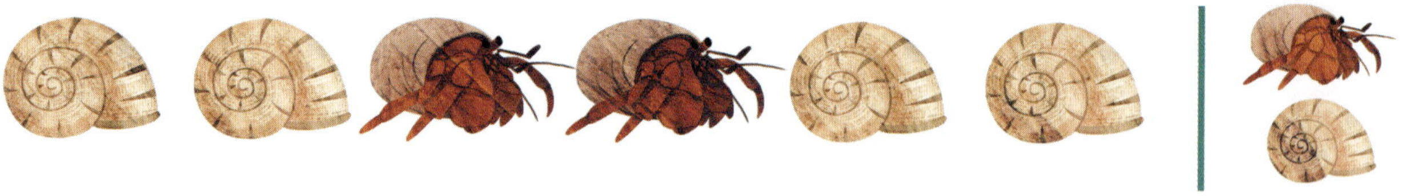

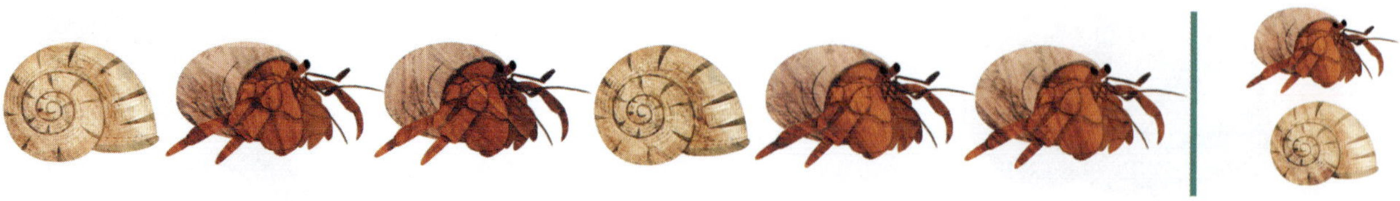

Sorting Shells

Sort the shells by color. Draw a line to show which sand pail each shell goes in.

Lighting Up the Deep

Some ocean creatures glow! The anglerfish has a body part that glows like a lightbulb.

EARLY CONCEPTS

Light the Way

Help the anglerfish find its way to the cave. Draw the path from the fish to the cave.

? A lanternfish's whole body can glow. Why do you think that happens?

Tracing Time

These lanternfish have rhyming words on their bodies! What is the beginning, middle, and ending sound of each word? Trace the letters as you say their sounds.

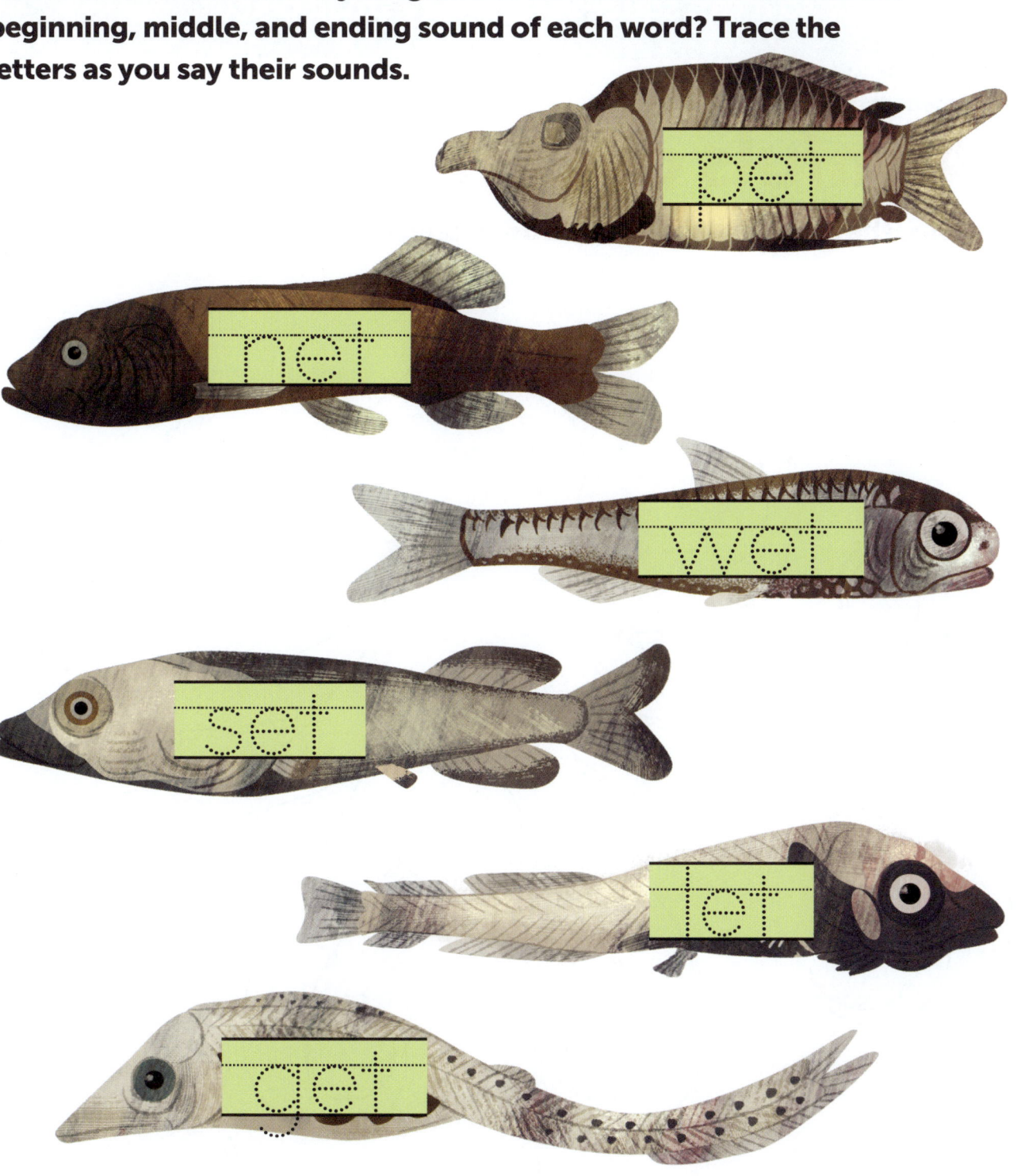

Marvelous Octopus

An octopus has eight arms and three hearts! It does not have bones, so it can squeeze into very small places.

LETTERS

Armfuls of Letters

Color the octopus. What sound does each letter make?

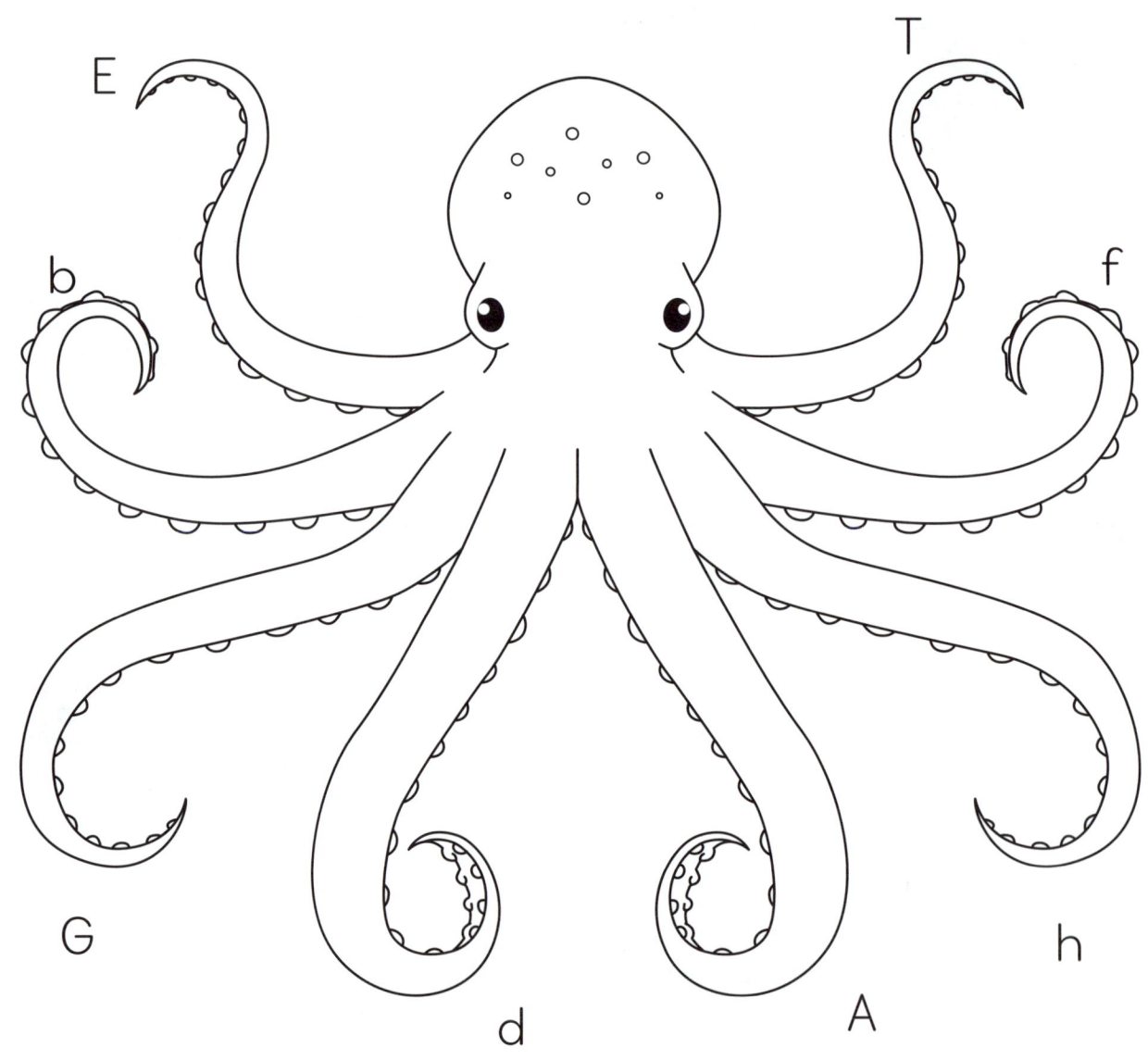

Finish the Picture

Draw the missing arms on the octopus. How many did you draw? Then color the octopus.

A Final Splash

You read a lot about water in this chapter. What was something you learned about water that you never knew before?

MATH

A Watery Leap

What animal jumps high out of the water and dives back in again? Connect the dots in the right order from 1 to 10 to find out.

8 9 10

7.

6.

5.

4.
3 2 1

Scuba Dive!

Scuba divers can go deep underwater. They can see many different plants and animals!

What does the scuba diver see? Draw what the diver might be looking at.

CHAPTER 6

Meet the Mammals

Did you know that both you and these quokkas are mammals? In this chapter, you'll learn about what makes mammals special. As you read, think about how you are like other mammals and how you are different.

Quokkas can use their strong back legs to hop like a rabbit!

Hello, Mammals!

Mammals are animals with fur or hair. The babies drink their mother's milk. Mammals may live in the water or on land.

LETTERS **WRITING**

M is for Mammal

Can you write **mammal**? Copy each letter into the boxes below. How many times did you write the letter **m**?

Humpback whales do have hair, but it's hard to see!

m   a   m   m   a   l

EARLY CONCEPTS | MATH

Find the Mammal

Do you remember what makes an animal a mammal? Find and circle the **5** mammals.

Furry Friends

A mammal's hair or fur can be thick and long or short and thin. It comes in many colors and patterns.

LETTERS

Pick the Letters

Color only the boxes with the letters that are used in the word **FUR**.

Sea otters have the thickest fur of any mammal.

G	F	O
U	M	R

136

Whose Fur Is It?

Circle the animal that matches the fur.

tiger   lion

bear   leopard

red panda   koala

walrus   goat

Stick Together

Some mammals live together in groups called herds. They work as a team to find food, raise babies, and keep each other safe.

LETTERS **WRITING**

Who Needs the Herd?

All of these animals live in herds.

Trace the first letter of each animal's name. What sound does the letter make?

eer

ippo

uffalo

LETTERS

Catch Up!

A herd of zebras is called a dazzle.

This animal needs to catch up to the herd.

Connect the dots in the right order from A to Z to find out who it is.

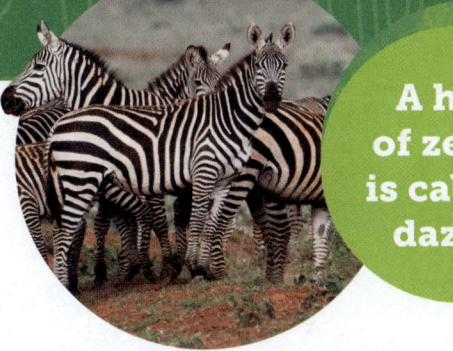

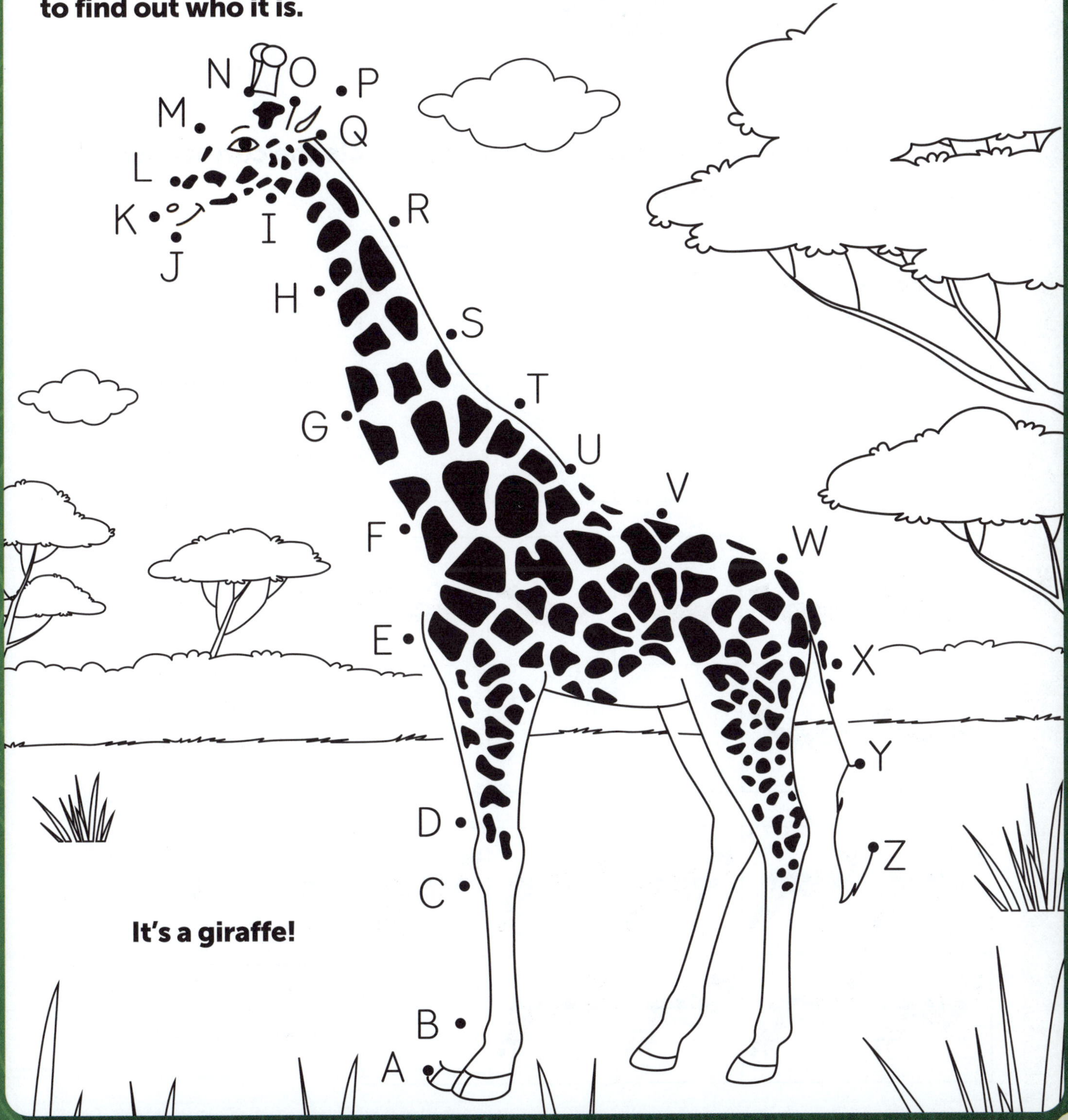

It's a giraffe!

Name That Group

Lots of mammals live and travel in groups, but they are not always called herds. Some groups of animals have special names.

MATH **READING** **WRITING**

Always Together

Count the number of animals in each group. Circle the correct number. Then trace the name of the group.

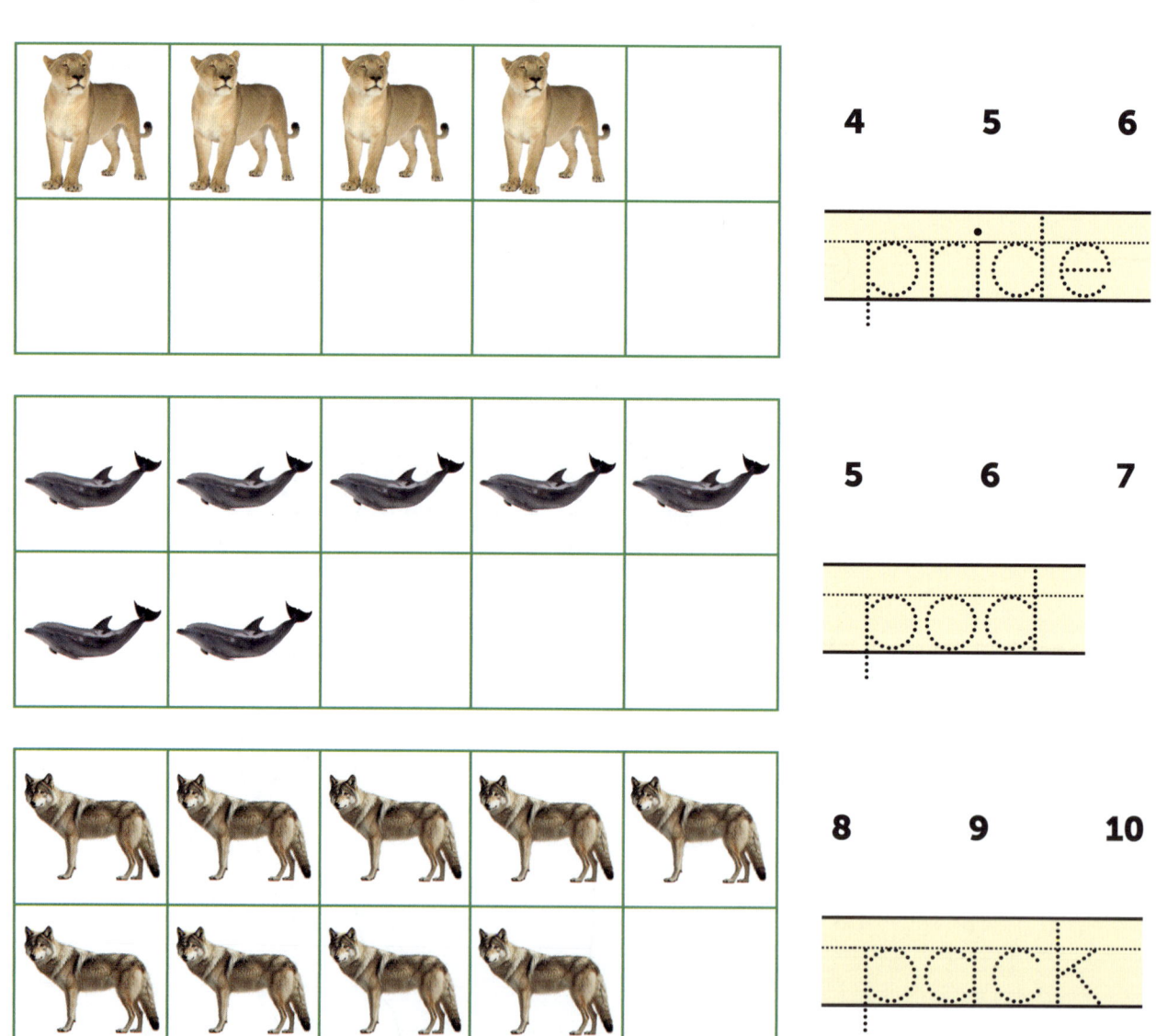

4   5   6

pride

5   6   7

pod

8   9   10

pack

lion pride

dolphin pod

wolf pack

flock of sheep

A A hot dog!

All Shapes and Sizes

Mammals can be big or small. The blue whale is the largest animal on Earth. The bumblebee bat can fit on the tip of your finger!

Big and Little

Circle the **biggest** mammal. Place a square around the **smallest** mammal.

? What is the biggest shape in the picture?

Bark! Bark!

Trace the color name next to each shape. Then look closely at the dog to find the shapes. Color each shape in the picture to match the colors of the shapes at the top.

143

Swinging Chimps!

Chimpanzees use their long arms to swing from tree branches. Their arms and the knuckles on their hands also help them walk!

MATH

Counting Chimps

Count the chimpanzees. Circle the number of chimps shown.

6   7   8

Chimps talk to each other by making faces. They also hoot, grunt, and scream!

Finding Home!

Chimps make nests high in trees.

Help the chimp find its nest. Lead it through the jungle.

END

145

Ocean Wonders

Whales can swim underwater for a long time, but they need to come up to the surface to breathe air.

narwhal

orca

READING

Whale Sounds

Circle the object that starts with the same letter sound as whale.

READING

Whale of a Rhyme!

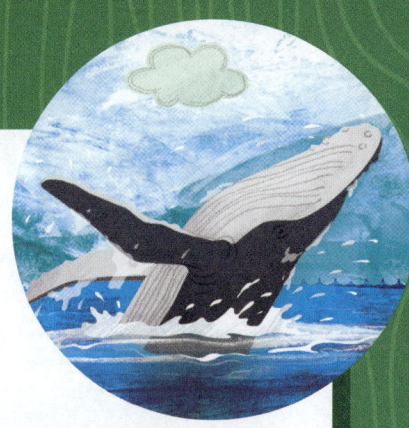

Say the word whale. Which body part of a whale rhymes with its name? Draw an X next to it.

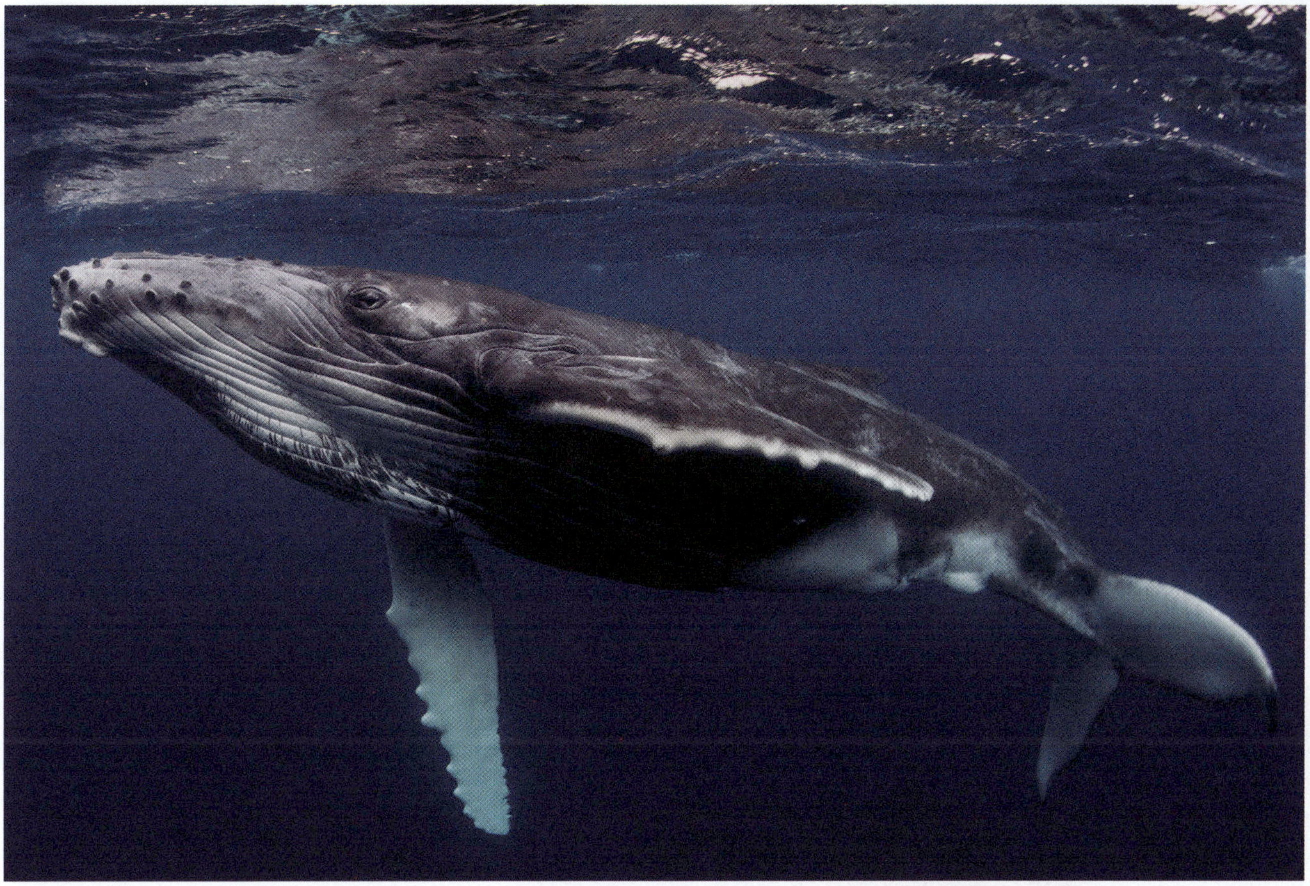

humpback whale

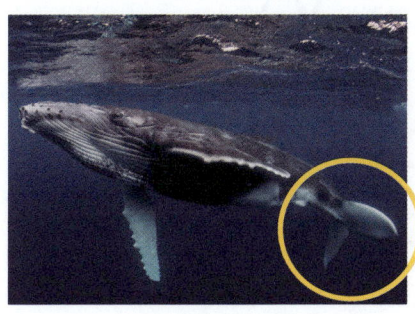

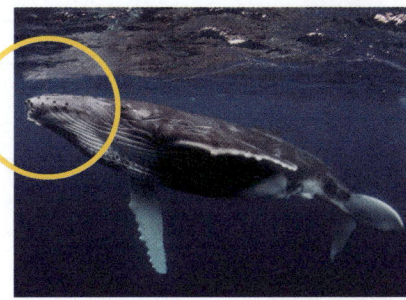

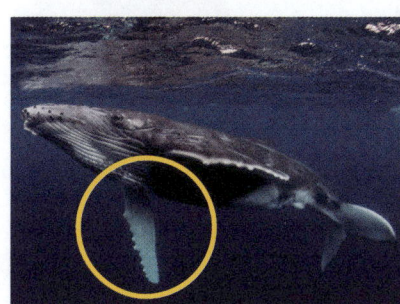

tail ☐

head ☐

flipper ☐

That Face!

Mammal faces can look really different, but most of them have two eyes, a nose, and a mouth—just like you!

rabbit

elephant

EARLY CONCEPTS　　**LETTERS**　　**WRITING**

Human Faces

Trace the first letter of each part of the face.

eye

ear

nose

mouth

148

Whose Face Is This?

Look at each face, then choose the animal it belongs to.

horse

giant panda

fox

bear

moose

orangutan

Where's Baby?

Most mammals give birth to live babies. This means their babies don't hatch from eggs. Usually they look a lot like their parents!

READING **WRITING**

Baby Names

Baby animals often have special names.

Trace the name for each baby animal. What is the beginning and ending sound of each name?

A baby bear is a cub.

A baby deer is a fawn.

A baby goat is a kid.

Mommy Matching

Uh-oh, the mom and baby animals got separated!

Draw a line to help match each mother with its baby.

Kittens are born with their eyes closed. It can take up to 16 days for them to open.

Jump, Kangaroo!

Kangaroo babies live in a pouch on their mom's belly. They don't leave the pouch at all until they are about four months old.

In or Out?

Some of these kangaroo babies, called joeys, are still inside their mother's pouch. Some of the joeys are outside the pouch.

Circle the joeys that are inside the pouch.

Hop to It

Kangaroos are great jumpers.

Circle the kangaroos that are jumping.

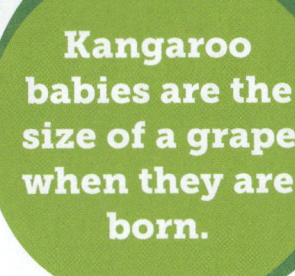

Powerful Polar Bears

Polar bears are Arctic mammals. They have a thick layer of fat called blubber. It keeps them warm even in freezing ocean water!

MATH

Cub Counting

Count the polar bear cubs. Circle the correct number.

6   7   8

Icy Alphabet

Write the alphabet in order from **A** to **Z** on the chunks of ice. Some of the letters are already there!

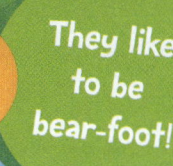

A → ___ ___ D
E ___ G G
___ ___ L L
___ N S ___
___ ___ S ___
___ ___ W
___ Y ___

155

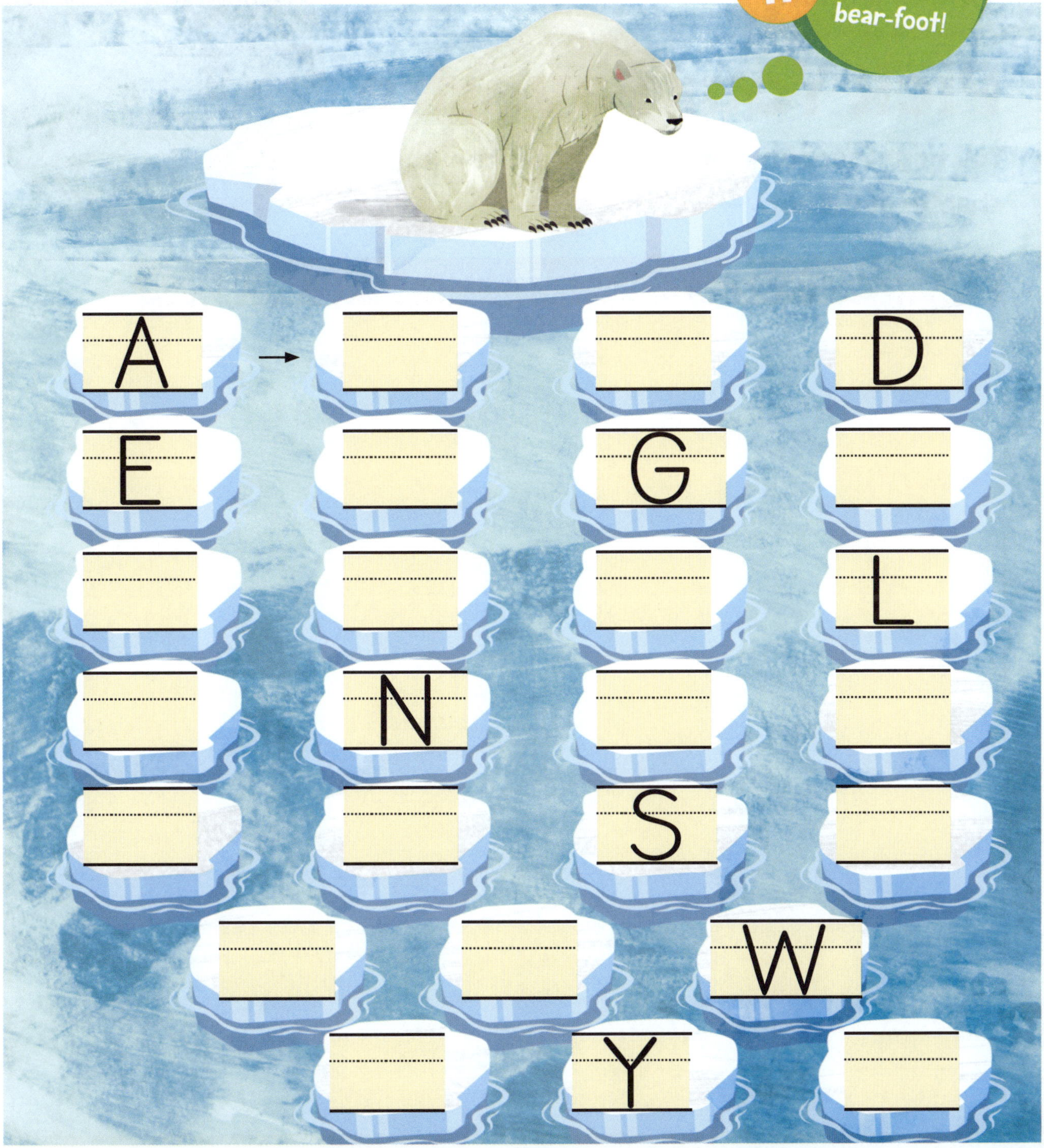

Zoo Mammals

A zoo can be a good place to watch wild mammals. Scientists also study animals in zoos.

Pick Your Favorite

You might see some of the mammals from this chapter at the zoo.

Which animal would you like to see at the zoo? Draw it here.

What Will I See There?

Here are some mammals you might see at a zoo.

Trace the first letter of each animal's name. What sound does it make?

tiger

elephant

bear

monkey

hippopotamus

Mammals and Me

You learned so much about mammals in this chapter. You even learned that you are a mammal!

EARLY CONCEPTS

Just Like Me

Think about which mammal is most like you. Draw it. Then tell someone why you picked it.

Caring for Mammals

Some mammals are our pets.

Connect the dots in the right order from 1 to 20 to see one way people take care of pets.

CHAPTER 7

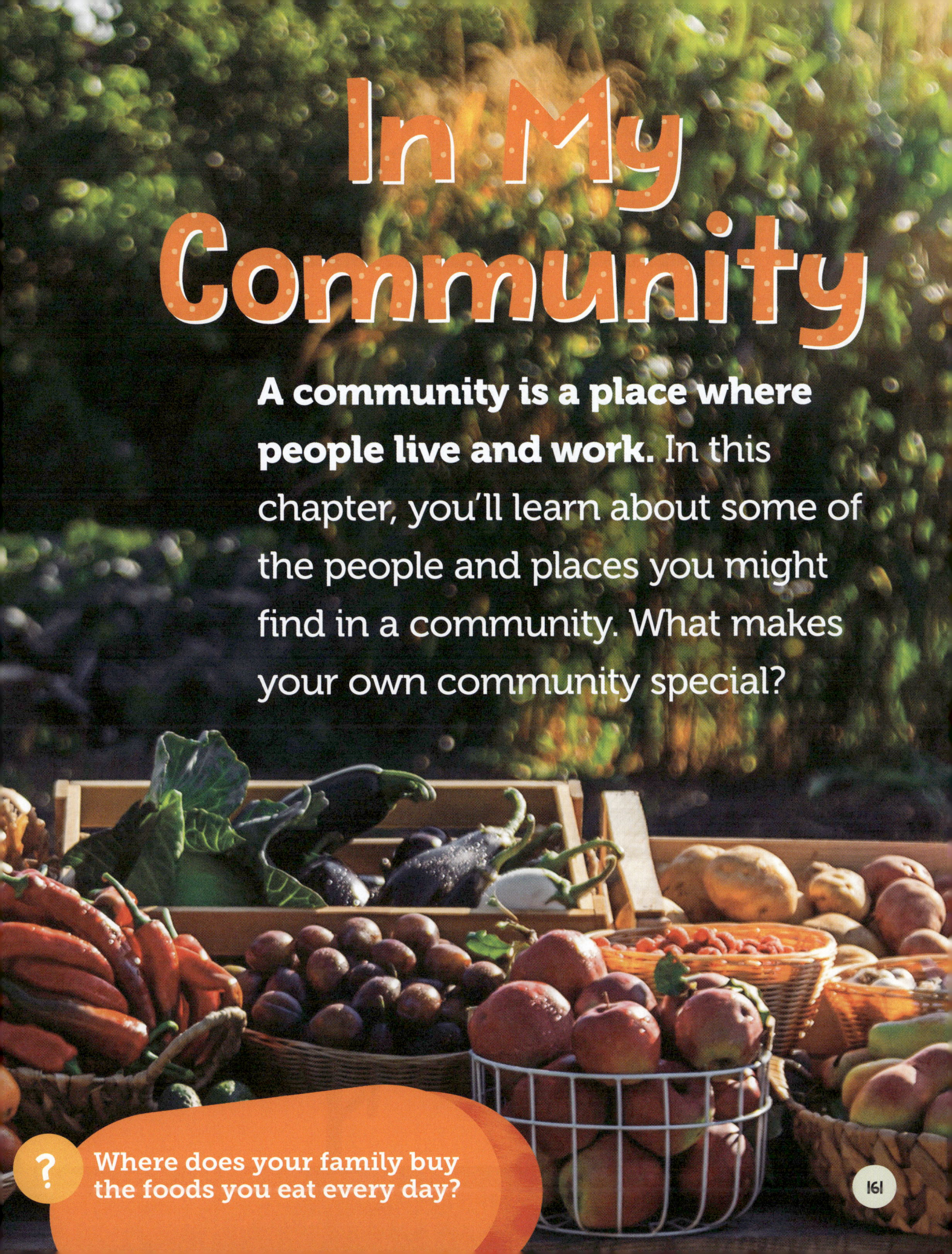

In My Community

A community is a place where people live and work. In this chapter, you'll learn about some of the people and places you might find in a community. What makes your own community special?

? Where does your family buy the foods you eat every day?

Come Out to Play!

Many communities have playgrounds and parks. They are places to run and play! Playgrounds bring people together.

What Starts With P?

What starts with **p** as in **play**? Circle the objects.

Play and Count

Count the bikes, benches, and swings. How many are there in all? Circle the number below the picture.

Exercise is good for your brain! It helps put you in a good mood.

11   12   13

Happy Hometowns

Where is your community? Is your home in a small town, or is it in a big city? People live in all kinds of places!

MATH

On the Map

A map is a special kind of picture that shows where things are.

Look at this map of a town. How many houses do you count? Circle the number.

8   9   10

READING   **WRITING**

Town and City

Trace the letters to form the words **town** and **city**.

   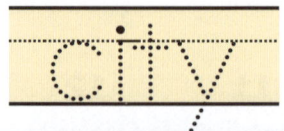

City Life

In cities, many people live in apartments.

See the windows on the apartments below?
Every window is a rectangle. Trace 4 windows.

More than half the people in the world live in cities. Do you live in a city?

Treasure Hunt!

What can you find in a town? You can find schools, grocery stores, homes, and more. But do you think you could find treasure?

Find the Treasure

Follow the dotted line. Start at home. End at the treasure!

What Is Inside?

What could be inside the treasure chest? Draw your ideas.

? Do you have a special box where you keep your treasures?

Police Helpers

Q Why did the police officer arrest the baseball player? ↪

A police officer's job is to help people stay safe. Some police officers drive in cars. Some ride bicycles. Some even ride horses!

MATH

Look for the Badge

How can you tell someone is a police officer? Look for their badge.

Connect the dots in the right order from 1 to 20 to see the police badge.

Taller and Bigger

Look at the picture. Circle the police officer that is **taller**. Circle the police motorcycle that is **bigger**.

A He stole third base!

Thanks, Firefighters!

Firefighters put out fires. They use hoses that spray water on the fire. They help people and animals who are in danger.

MATH | **WRITING**

Stop, Drop, and Roll

If your clothes catch fire, stop! Drop to the floor and lie down.

Then roll over. Keep rolling until the fire is out.

Put the pictures in order from 1 to 3. Write the numbers in the boxes.

MATH

Teamwork

Firefighters work as a team.

How many firefighters do you see? Count them. Circle the number.

A They carry their own hoses!

6   7   8

Mail Time

Mail carriers deliver letters and packages. They stop at each home to deliver mail. What kind of mail comes to your home?

Deliver the Mail

Help deliver the mail! Follow the dotted mail route. Trace the mailboxes to deliver mail at each home.

Letters on Letters

Trace the letters on each piece of mail. Choose letters to write on the last two.

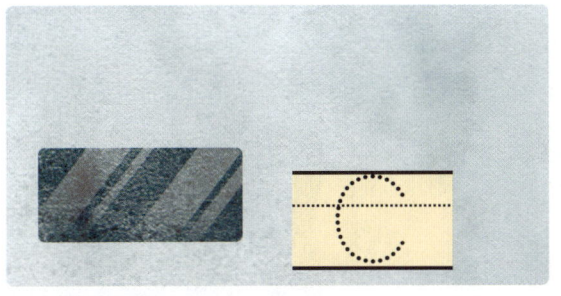

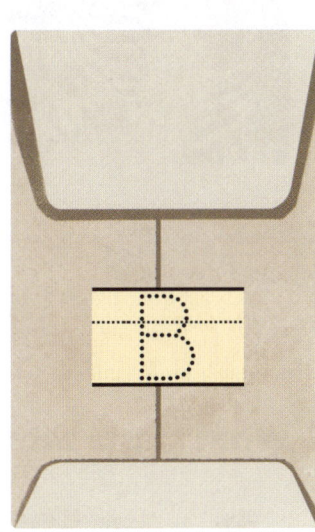

Hooray for Teachers!

Teachers are important community helpers. They teach us math, reading, and writing. They teach us how to get along!

LETTERS

What Starts With T?

What starts with t for teacher? Circle it.

LETTERS **WRITING**

What's Missing?

Trace the first and last letters in the word teacher. What sound does each letter make?

In the Classroom

Circle **4** things you might find in a classroom.

Going to School

Schools are an important part of a community. You can learn new things in school. You can meet new friends there, too!

School Activities

What things do you do at school? Circle them.

Find the Bus!

Many school buses go to school.

Find the bus with the number 6. Color it yellow.

Signs Around Town

Signs tell people and cars where to go and what to do.
Can you think of some signs you see around your community?

Which Way?

This sign tells cars which way to go.

Draw a line from each letter on the sign to the matching lowercase letter below.

e   n   o   y   w   a

Stop!

Trace the letters to write the word stop.
Then color the picture. Color the stop sign red.

A Helping Hand

We can all help take care of our community! We can pick up trash. We can use less plastic. We can recycle.

Keep Recycling!

Look at the pattern. What comes next? Circle it.

Will It Help?

Look at each picture. Does it help or hurt the community? Point to the happy face for help or the sad face for hurt.

A Place for Friends

A community is a place where you can make friends. You can learn from friends and spend time together. You can explore and play!

MATH   **WRITING**

Friend Count

Count the friends. Write the number on the line below.

There are  friends.

EARLY CONCEPTS | MATH

It Takes 2

It only takes 2 people to make a friendship.

Draw 2 friends: yourself and a friend from your community.

See You Around!

You learned about some of the helpers in your community. Who else helps in your community? Where can you find them in your town?

Hometown Heroes

Color the pictures of the helpers in a community.

Bus drivers help.

Doctors and nurses help.

Lifeguards help.

Crossing guards help.

Your Own Hero

Q Why did the banana go to the doctor?

Who is a hero in your community? Draw yourself with the person.

A It wasn't peeling well!

CHAPTER 8

Prairie dogs live together in large underground homes called towns.

Home Sweet Home

From snowy mountains to dry deserts and deep oceans, animals can live almost anywhere! In this chapter, you'll explore the many different places animals make their homes.

At Home

A habitat is an area where an animal can find everything it needs to survive, like food and shelter. The habitat for many monkeys is the rainforest. An animal's home is the specific place where it lives. Some monkeys make their homes in trees!

habitat

home

READING **WRITING**

Write It Out

Trace the word **homes**. What sounds do you hear at the beginning and end?

Howler monkeys use their tails to grip tree branches.

188

Tiger Homes

Find the letters that make up the word homes. Color only those boxes.

H	L	O
M	E	K
U	J	S

Dry, Dry Deserts

A desert is a very dry habitat. Desert plants and animals need little water. Deserts get less than 10 inches (25 cm) of rain all year!

Funny Faces

Many animals live in the desert.

Draw a line to match one side of each desert animal's face to the other side.

Desert Discovery

Draw a check mark next to the pictures that show a desert.

Desert Friends

Draw a check mark next to 2 animals that live in the desert.

camel

dolphin

duck

sand gazelle

Brr, It's Cold!

Some habitats are very cold. Animals in these places live right on the snow and ice. They can find food there!

READING   **WRITING**

Icy Words

Look! There are rhyming words on the floating ice. Trace each word.

bat

sat

hat

mat

pat

Waddling Penguin

The penguin wants to go for a swim.

Help the penguin walk across the ice to the ocean water.

Like all birds, penguins have feathers. They can't fly, but they are awesome swimmers!

END

Life Under the Sea

Most of our planet is covered by ocean! The ocean is the largest habitat on Earth, and huge numbers of animals live there.

Totally Turtles

Count the number of sea turtles in each group. Circle the number.

6   7   8

3   4   5

? How many ocean animals can you think of? Have you seen any in real life?

Ocean Neighbors

Here are just a few animals that live in the ocean.

Trace the first letter of each animal's name. What sound does the letter make?

Seal

lobster

crab

Sea star

dolphin

octopus

195

A Grassy Home

Many plants and animals live in grasslands. These are huge fields of grass. The grass there can be as tall as you are!

EARLY CONCEPTS

Powerful Cats

The tiger's stripes make a pattern.

Circle the next color in the orange-and-black pattern.

Counting Stripes

Circle the number of black stripes on each zebra.

8   9   10

3   4   5

6   7   8

7   8   9

Rain Again?

It's raining! Rainforests get more rain than any other place on Earth. Plants and animals there need lots of water to live and grow.

Drips and Drops

Look! The raindrops have letters inside them. Color the drops that have lowercase letters.

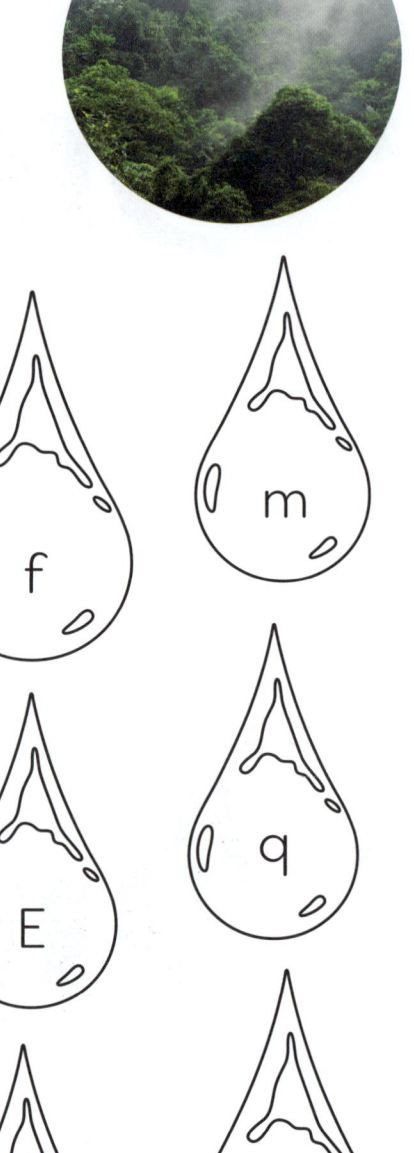

D

Y

b

f

m

A

g

E

q

R

k

P

t

J

198

Who's There?

This hairy fellow lives in the rainforest.

Who is it? Connect the dots from 1 to 20 to find out.

Chocolate comes from a plant that grows in the rainforest.

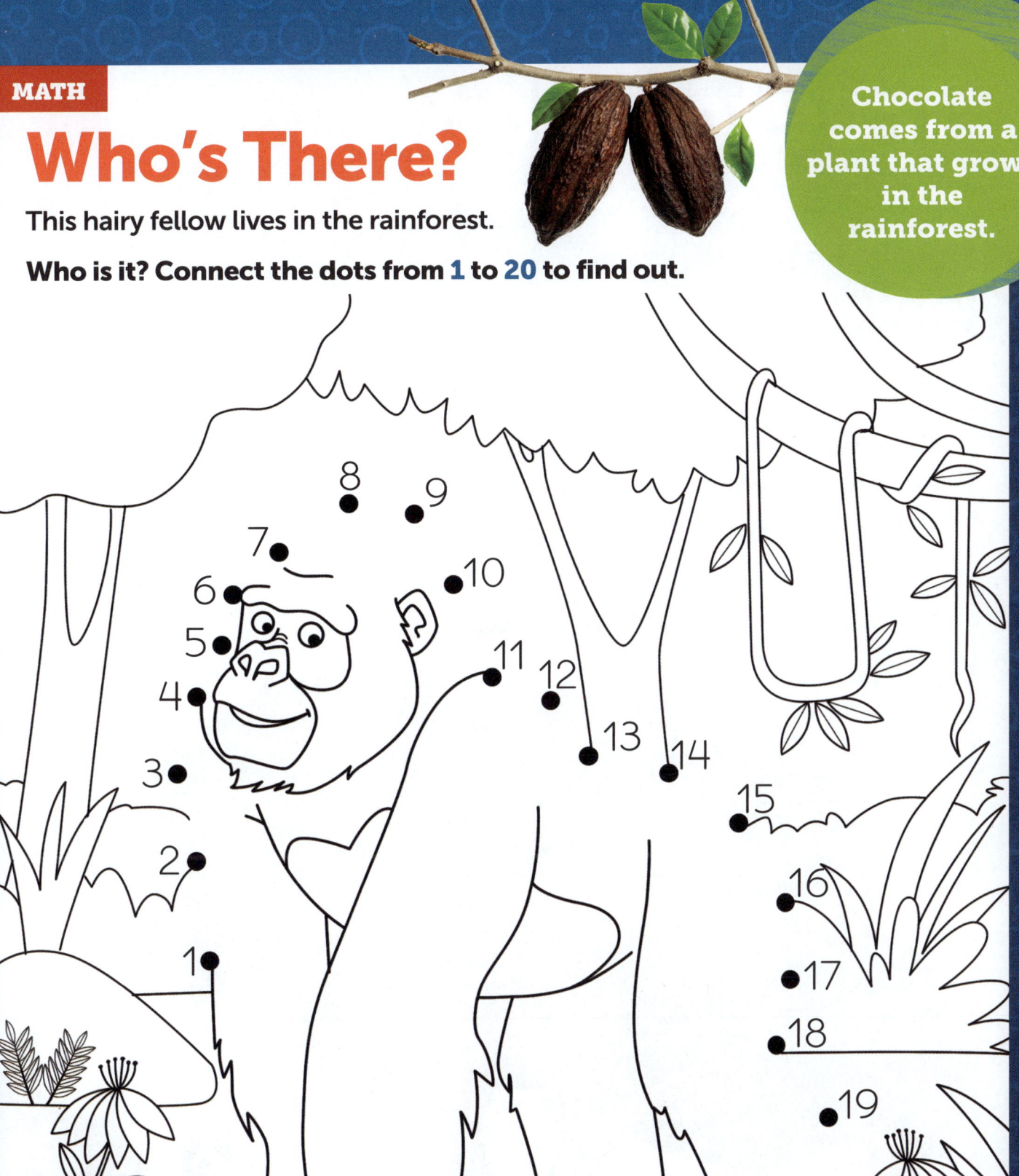

Treetop Homes

Animals may make homes high up in trees. This can help keep them safe from predators.

Friends of the Tree

Color the animal **inside** the tree. Circle the animal **on** the tree. Put a square around the animal **next to** the tree. Make an **X** on the animal **over** the tree.

MATH

Up in the Branches

Some bees build their homes in trees. These homes are called nests.

Count the bees. Circle the correct number.

8   9   10

READING   **WRITING**

A Happy Home

The monkeys are at home in the tree.

Trace the word home.

We are glad to be

home !

Nesting Time

Many animals make their home in a nest. Babies stay in a nest as they grow. Then they leave the nest and go out on their own.

EARLY CONCEPTS | **WRITING**

Welcome, Babies

Meet the duck-billed platypus! It builds a nest, then it lays eggs in the nest. When the eggs hatch, the young stay safe in the nest.

Which picture happens first? Put the pictures in order from 1 to 4. Write the number underneath each picture.

Uppercase Eggs

The eggs in this nest have letters on them!

Color the eggs that have uppercase letters.

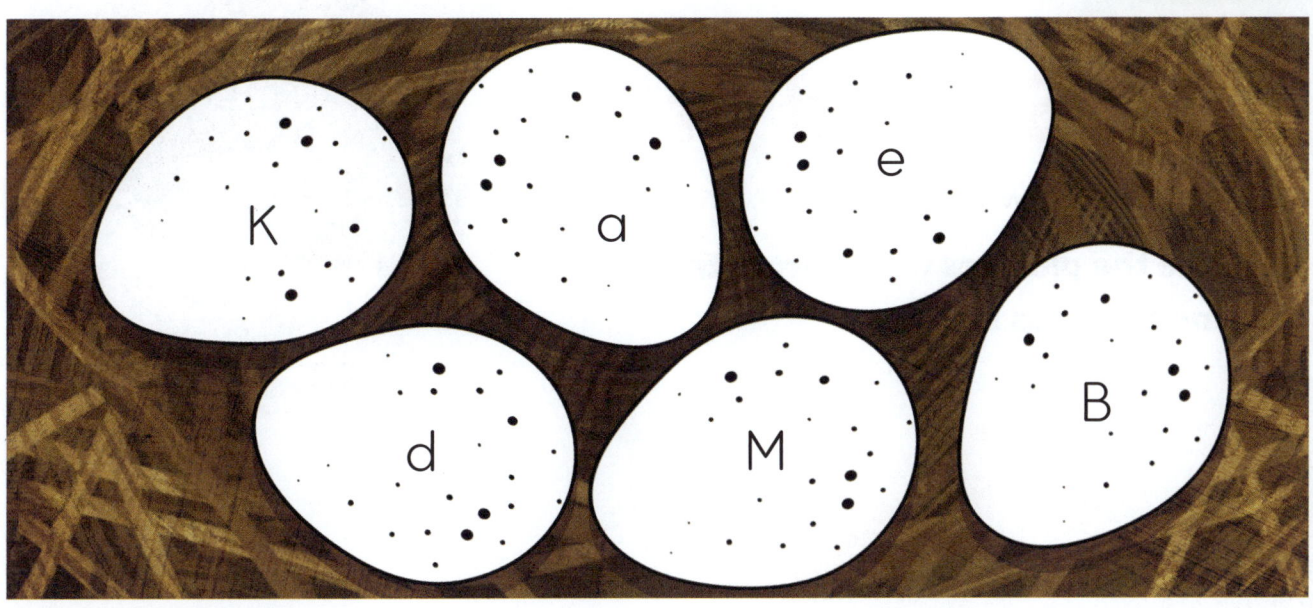

Who's Home?

Which animal do you think made this nest and lives in it?

ant

squirrel

horse

bear

Under Your Feet

Some animals make homes underground. An underground home is called a burrow. Would you be cozy in an underground home?

The Sound of B

Burrow starts with the letter b.

Circle the pictures that start with the same sound as burrow.

Burrowing Buddies

More animals are coming home to the burrow!

Count each type of animal and write how many there are in all.

+

=

   +  =

 +  =

 +  =

Peek Inside a Cave

Caves are large holes in the earth. They can be safe homes for animals. Have you ever seen a cave or the animals that live there?

MATH

Bat Search

Time for a rest!

There are bats hanging upside down in the cave. Color 4 of them.

How many bats are there in the picture above? How many more bats are needed so there are 10 in all? Draw them in the box below.

Who's Inside?

? Why do you think some animals make their homes inside caves?

These animals live in caves.

Trace the last letter in each name. What is the last sound in each name?

oilbird

swiftlet

salamander

MATH

Growl!

The bears have woken up from their long nap.

How many bears are there? Circle the number.

5   6   7

Walking Home

Look closely! Do you see footprints? Animals moving around their habitat might leave footprints in the snow, mud, or sand.

Trekking Tracks

Look at each set of animal tracks. Circle the next footprint in the pattern.

Where Do They Live?

Draw a line from each animal and its footprint to the habitat where it lives.

Human Habitats

People live in habitats, too. Cities and towns are habitats for people! Homes for people may be houses or apartment buildings.

LETTERS   **WRITING**

A Path Home

There are letters on the path to the house!

Complete the missing letters in the pattern.

A

B

___

D

___

___

G

___

Gardens at Home

Many people grow food in their gardens at home.

Circle the food that is the same as the first one in the row.

Homes for All

You learned all about the habitats where animals live. They can be wet or dry. They can be hot or cold. Animals make their homes in trees, deep in caves, and even underground!

Draw It!

Think of 2 different animal homes you learned about. Draw them.

Who Lives Here?

What animal makes its home in the woods? Connect the dots in the right order from 1 to 20 to find out. Then color the picture.

CHAPTER 9

Brilliant Birds

You hear a rustle in the leaves or a song overhead. What could be making those sounds? A bird! Birds are all around us. You might see one flying through the sky or hopping across the ground. In this chapter, you'll learn what makes these animals special.

? Do you know the name of this bird? Here's a hint: Its tail changes to show a big surprise!

It's a Bird!

All birds have some things in common. What could those things be? Birds have beaks, wings, and feathers, and they lay eggs.

LETTERS **WRITING**

On the Ground

Even though all birds have wings, not all birds can fly. Here are **3** birds that walk instead of fly.

Trace the first letters of their names. What sound does each letter make?

Penguin

Emu

Cassowary

An emu can run at about 30 miles an hour (48 km/h)!

MATH **WRITING**

How Many Eggs?

Bird eggs come in different sizes and colors.

Write numbers 1 to 10 on the eggs.

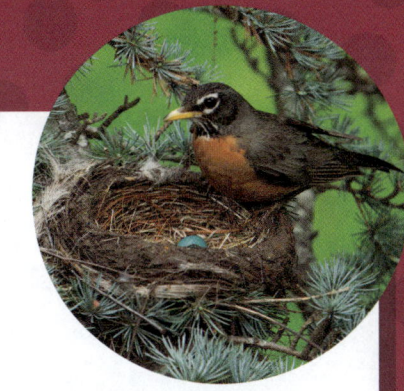

robin

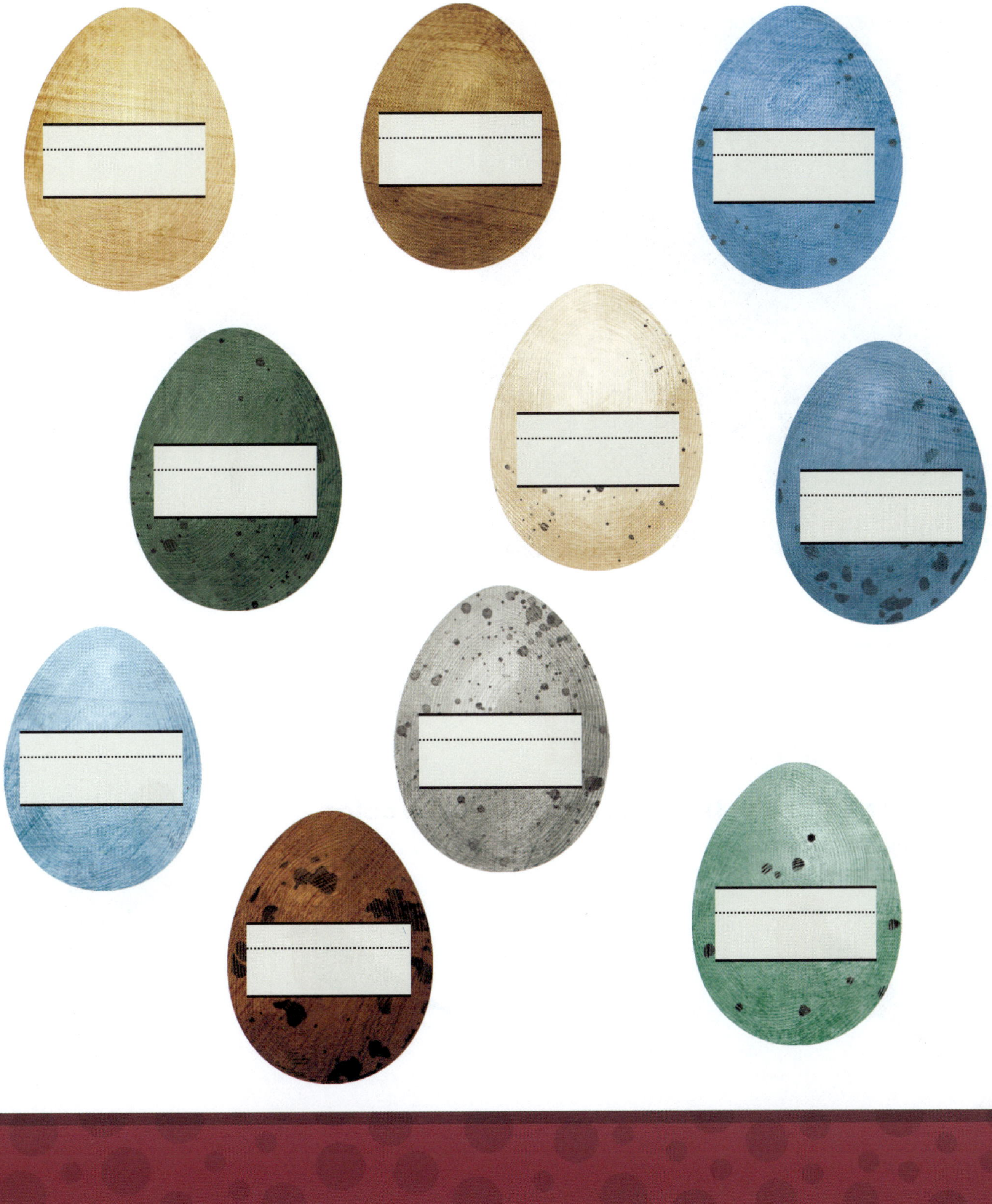

A Flap of Color

Birds come in all different colors. Some of them are very bright colors, like these!

toucan

flamingo

A flamingo turns bright pink when it eats a lot of shrimp!

EARLY CONCEPTS

An Odd Bird

Draw an **X** on the bird that is not the same color as the others.

Color Match

Find the crayon that matches the color of each bird.
Draw lines to connect them.

Feathers in Flight

Why do birds have feathers? Feathers help birds fly. They protect their skin. They even keep the birds warm and dry.

Feathery Sounds

Circle the things that start with the same beginning sound as feather.

EARLY CONCEPTS

Make It Your Own

Many birds have beautiful feathers. Some are colorful.

Some have dots. Some have stripes or patterns.

Decorate this feather. Be creative!

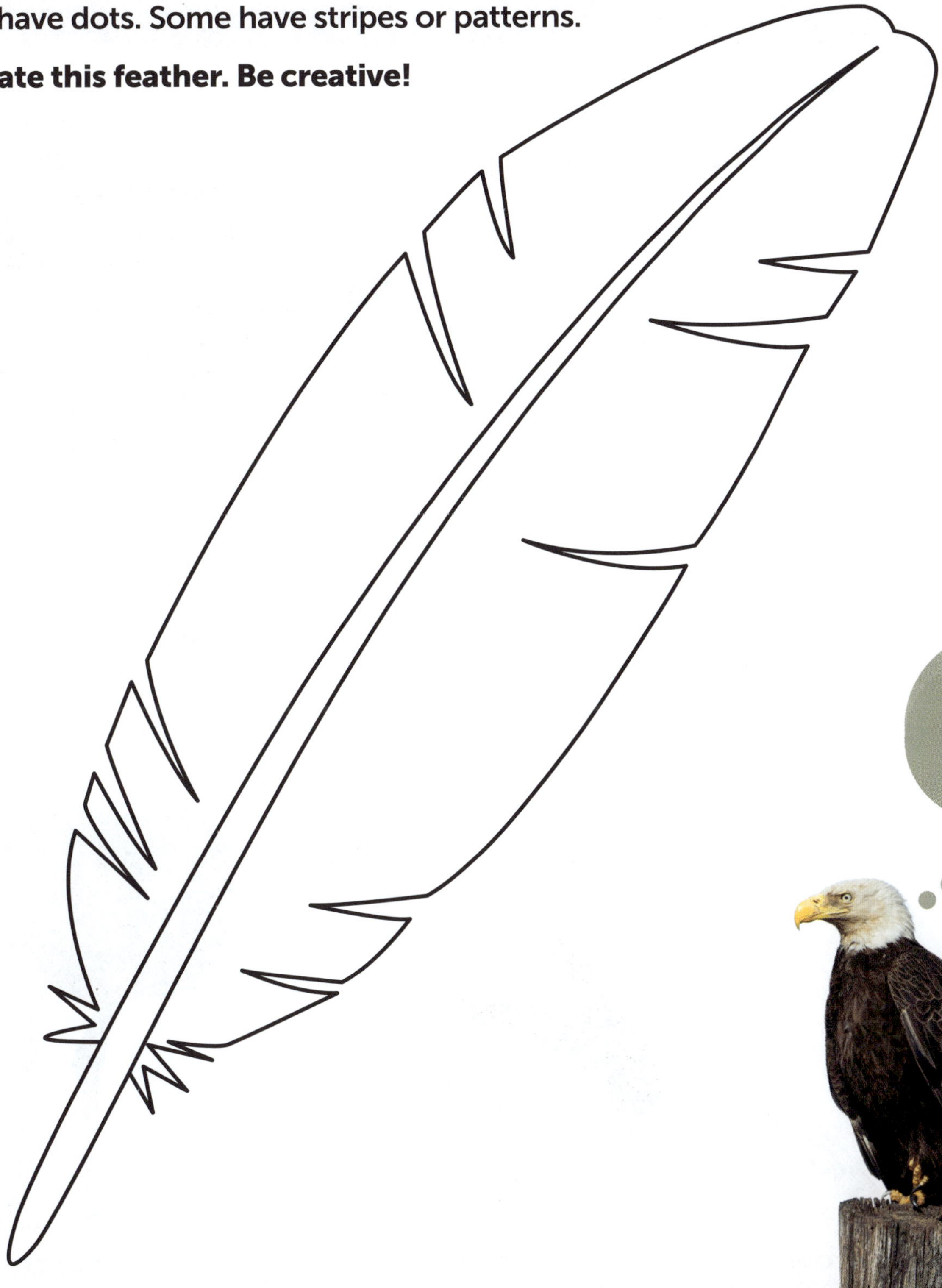

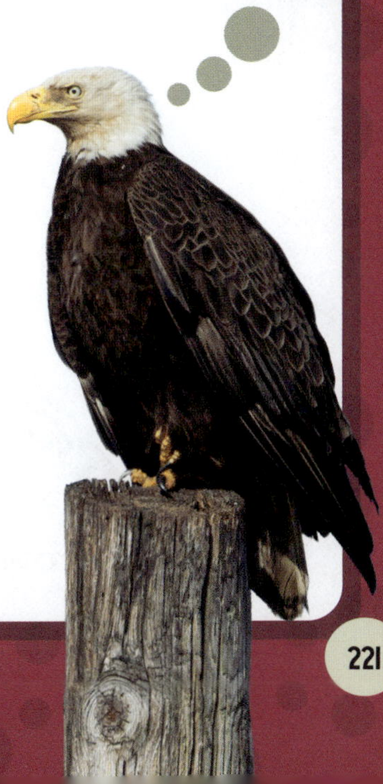

A bald eagle!

A

221

Open Your Beak!

A bird's beak is the hard part of its mouth. Birds can use their beaks for many things. What does this bird have in its beak?

Find the Letters

Color the squares with letters that are in **BEAK**.

M	B	E
A	S	K

EARLY CONCEPTS

Long or Short?

Which bird has the longest beak?
Which bird has the shortest legs?

sparrow

stork

ostrich

222

More and More Beaks

More birds mean more beaks!

There are no teeth in a bird's beak!

Draw **1** more bird with a beak. How many are there now? _____

Add **2** more birds with beaks. How many are there now? _____

Hop, Hop, Hooray!

Birds have different kinds of feet. A bird's feet might help it hop, grab, or swim. What do you think these feet are good for?

hawk

loon

Which Footprint Comes Next?

Look at the pattern. Which bird footprint comes next? Circle it.

A loon can't walk well on land! Its feet are too far back for walking, but they are great for swimming.

How Many Toes?

How many toes do you see? Write the number in the box.

The Nest Is Best

Birds lay their eggs in a nest. The babies stay in the nest as they grow. Then they learn to fly and find food on their own!

EARLY CONCEPTS | **MATH**

Home Sweet Home

Use the number key below to color each part of this bird.

yellow warbler

1 · 2 · 3 · 4

Feeding Time

Bird parents must leave the nest to find food.

Help the parent get the caterpillar to its babies!

Yellow warblers cover their nests with spiderweb silk to make them stronger.

A Ducky Day

Q What do you call a crate of ducks? →

Have you ever seen ducks at a pond? They look for food in the water. Ducks dunk their heads deep under the surface!

LETTERS

Flying Letters

Ducks fly in a **V** shape in the sky. Circle the picture that shows something that starts with a **V** sound.

Ducky Dots

Connect the dots in the right order from 1 to 15. Then color the picture.

A box of quackers!

A Good Egg

Most bird eggs are the shape of an oval. Hummingbirds lay the smallest eggs of any bird. Ostriches lay the largest eggs.

MATH

Eggy Shapes

**Which of these shapes could be eggs?
Color only the oval shapes.**

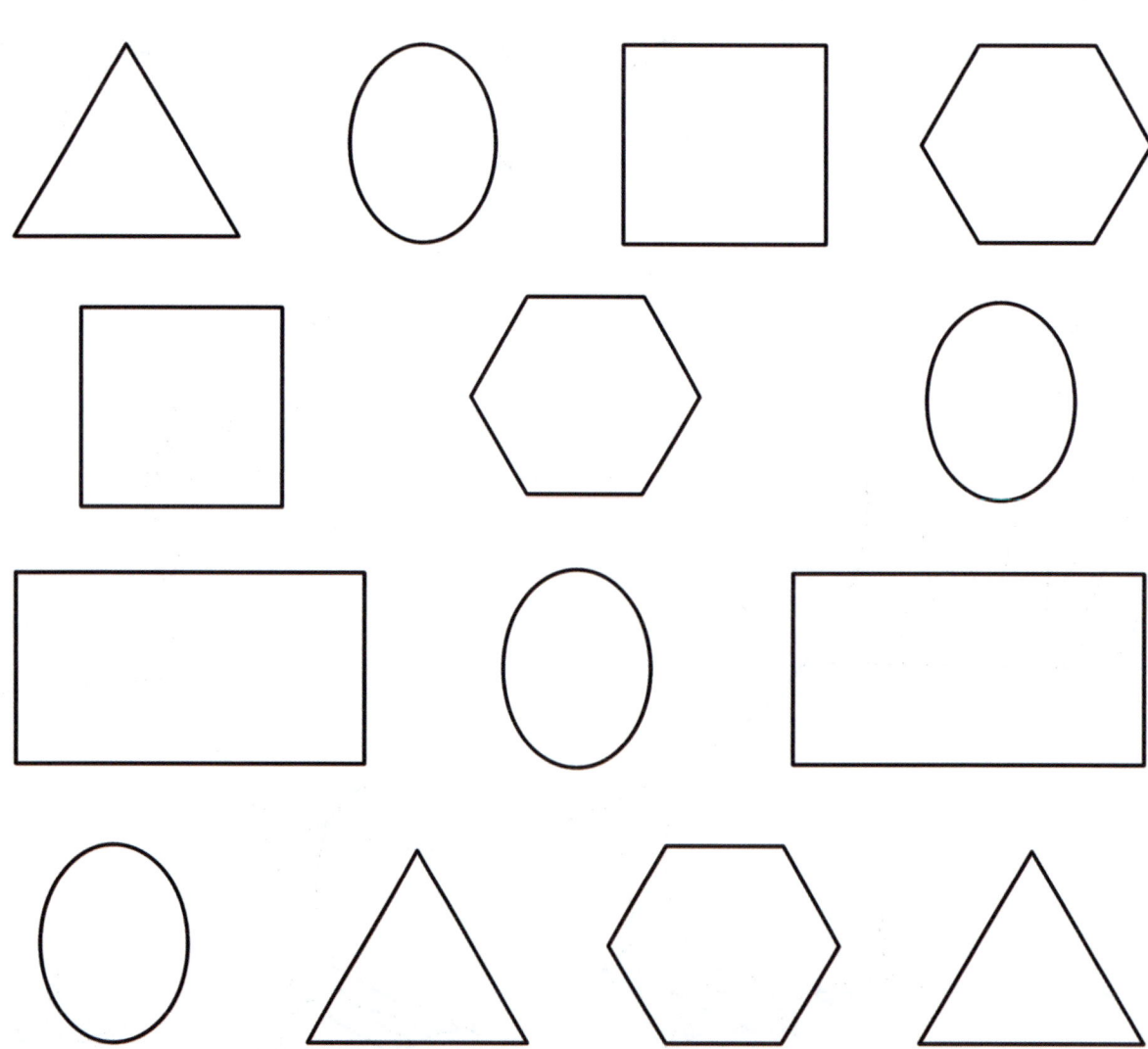

All in Order

Bird eggs come in all sizes.

**Number the eggs from smallest to largest.
Start with the number 1.**

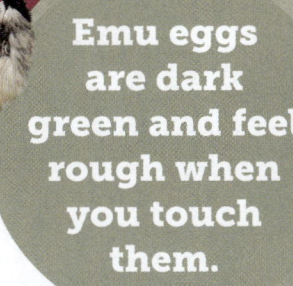

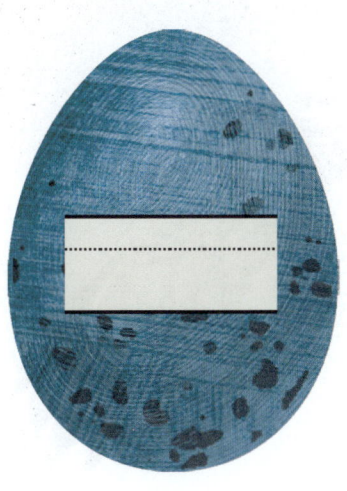

231

Time to Eat!

What do birds eat? Many eat seeds, nuts, and berries. Some eat worms and bugs or nectar from flowers. Some big birds eat fish!

EARLY CONCEPTS

Matching Pals

Find the **2** birds that are the same. Circle them.

MATH

Bird Food Counting

Count each type of bird food. Circle the number that tells how many there are of each type.

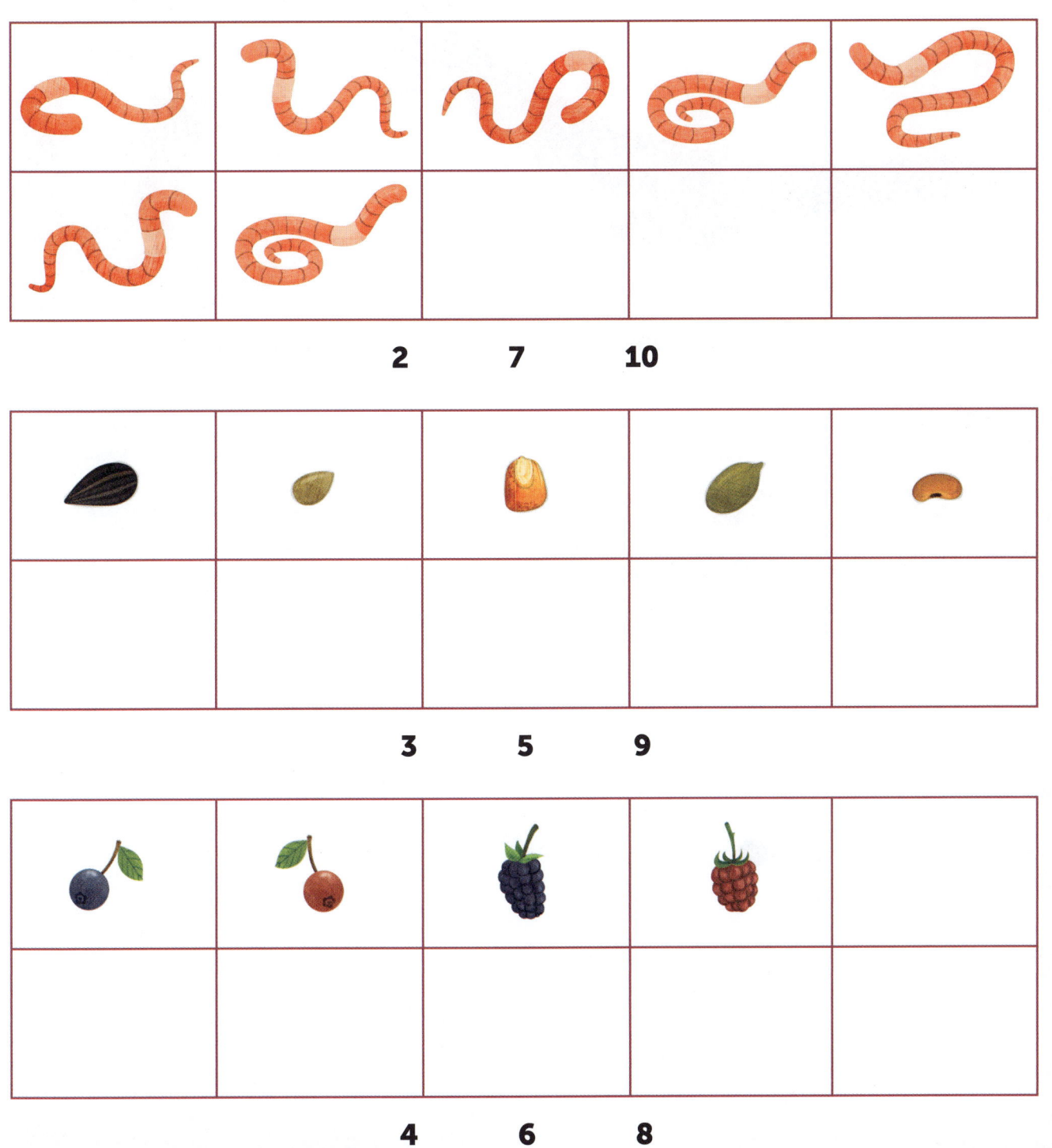

2   7   10

3   5   9

4   6   8

233

All Shapes and Sizes

Birds come in all shapes and sizes. The condor has huge wings! This hummingbird is one of the smallest birds in the world.

Andean condor

bee hummingbird

MATH

Bird Shapes

Look at the shapes that make up the bird. Trace each shape. Color each shape a different color.

A bee hummingbird weighs less than a dime!

234

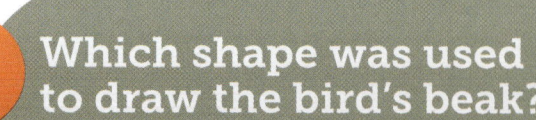

? Which shape was used to draw the bird's beak?

Who's the Biggest?

Circle the largest bird in each row.

Words About Birds

Trace the words in the sentence.

Birds   big  small!

235

Brainy Birds

Q What do you call a parrot that can't fly? →

Some birds are very smart. The bald eagle can crack ice with its beak. Then it jumps on the ice to break it. It's fishing time!

EARLY CONCEPTS

Imagine It!

People teach some birds to do tricks.

What tricks would you teach a bird? Draw and write about it.

Pretty Parrot!

Parrots are very smart! Some can count and add numbers.

Help this parrot add up the fruits for its snack.

A walkie-talkie.

 +  = _____

 +  = _____

 +  = _____

Bye-Bye, Birdie!

In this chapter, you learned all about our feathered friends. Some are huge, like a condor. Some are tiny, like a hummingbird. What else did you learn about birds?

EARLY CONCEPTS

All About Birds

Draw a picture to show what you learned about birds.

EARLY CONCEPTS

Showing Off!

This is the bird from the beginning of the chapter! Here, the peacock's beautiful tail feathers are spread out wide.

Color them any way you like.

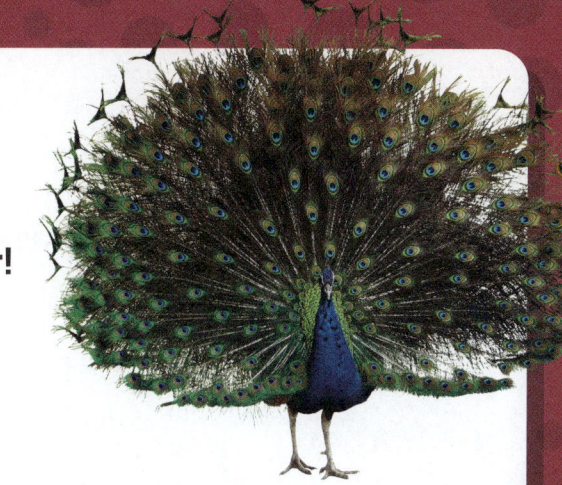

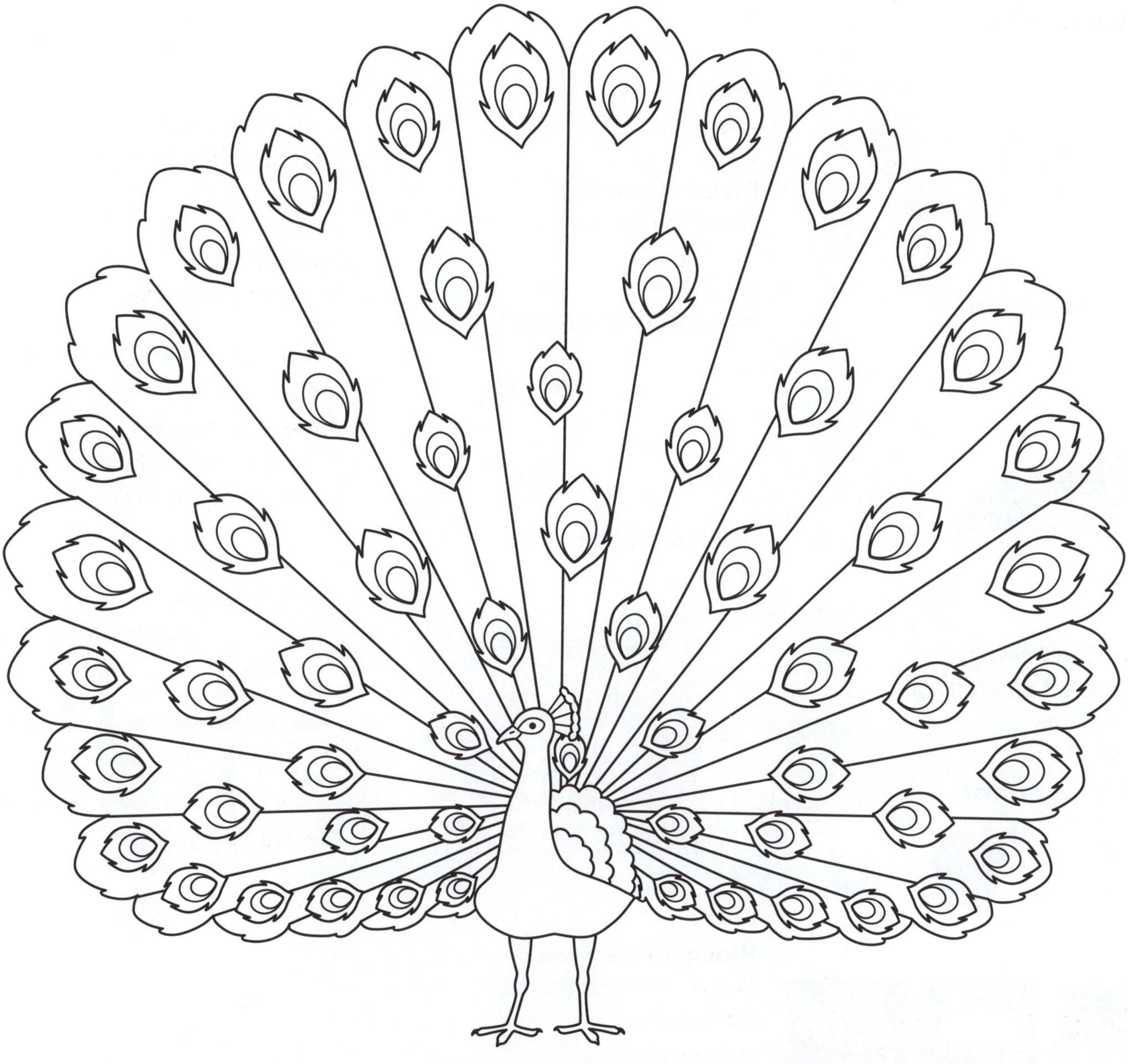

Answer Key

Chapter 1: Forest Friends

pp. 8–9

Where's the Fruit?

Colorful Apples

pp. 12–13

A Wiggly Pattern

Counting Crawlers
There are 3 caterpillars.

pp. 14–15

Go Home, Mama!

pp. 16–17

Where's the Eagle?

A Tasty Meal
The eagle ate 5 fish.

pp. 18–19

Plant Needs
The plant needs sunlight and water.

Forest Flowers
There are 6 flowers.

pp. 20–21

Who Looks the Same?

Back to the Burrow

pp. 22–23

Hiding in the Forest
The H is behind the tree branches.

On the Run
The 8 is missing from the picture.

pp. 24–25

What's in a Lodge?
Rocks, dirt, and sticks are in a lodge.

A Beaver Builds
The beaver will add 9 logs.

pp. 26–27

Growing Up

Count the Deer
There are 10 jumping deer.

pp. 28–29

Forest Pals
There are 7 animals.

Chapter 2: On the Farm

pp. 32–33

More Hay, Please!
The farmer has 9 bales of hay. Draw 1 more to make 10.

pp. 34–35

Lamb Matchup
The matching lambs are K and h.

Circles Everywhere

pp. 36–37
Milk to Share
There are 7 glasses of milk.
Back to the Barn

pp. 38–39
Egg Hunt

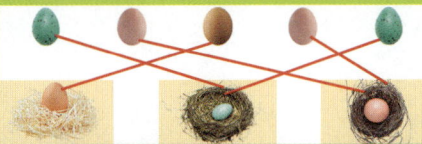

Picky Eaters

pp. 40–41
Farmer's Helpers
Circle the shovel, tractor, and rake.

Oooo … I See It!
Mark the overalls, orange, and oatmeal.

pp. 42–43
Pig Pals
There are 5 pigs.
A Standout Pig

pp. 44–45
Duck After Duck
There are 7 ducks in the top drawing. There are 9 ducks in the bottom drawing.

pp. 48–49
Piles of Corn

Silo Sight Words
Color the silos with the words "and," "as," and "at."

pp. 50–51
T Time
Mark "tree," "tortoise," and "tent."
Collect the Corn

pp. 52–53
Spot the Spots!
The cow has 7 spots. The pig has 4 spots. The horse has 4 spots.
Who Does Not Belong?

pp. 54–55
A Farmer's Friend

Chapter 3: Wonderful Weather
pp. 58–59
What Starts With V?

Lost in the Fog

pp. 60—61

Blow, Breeze, Blow!
Circle the beach ball, piece of paper, and feather.

Counting Clouds
She can see 5 clouds.

pp. 62—63

Which Is Wilder?

Tornado Count
2 groups of 10 tornadoes makes 20 tornadoes.

pp. 64—65

Summer Sun

What to Wear?

pp. 66—67

Count the Bolts
There are 4 lightning bolts.

pp. 68—69

Color Your Own

pp. 70—71

Missing Letters
The words are "cloud," "rain," and "drop."

Find the 4s

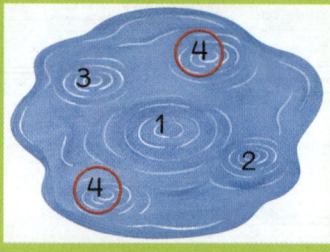

What Do We Need Today?

pp. 72—73

6 Points

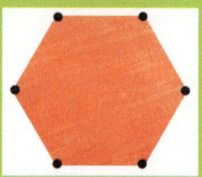

Snowflake Patterns

Snowflakes on My Head!

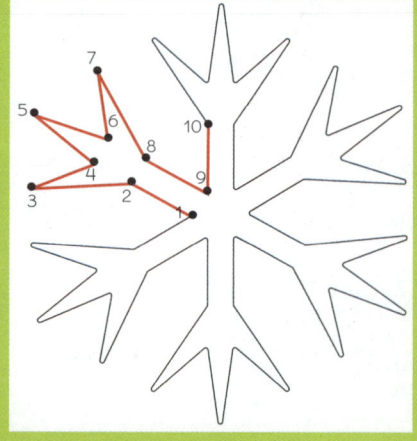

pp. 74—75

Playtime
Playing on the beach and swimming in the pool.

A Walk Through the Garden

Cloud Counter

Colorful Clouds
Color the clouds with "in," "if," and "it."

Draw the Forecast

Day	Forecast	Picture
Monday	Sunny	
Tuesday	Cloudy	
Wednesday	Rainy	
Thursday	Snowy	
Friday	Windy	

A Rainy Day Pal

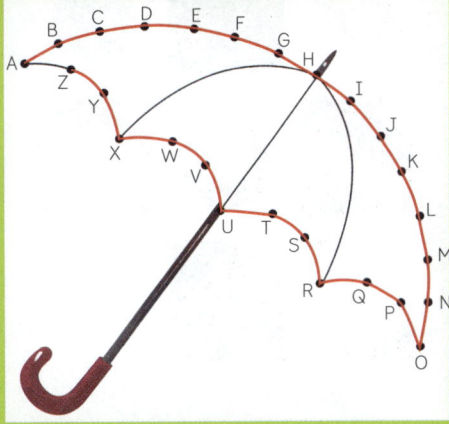

Chapter 4: Space Adventure

Rocket Shapes

Big Letter, Little Letter

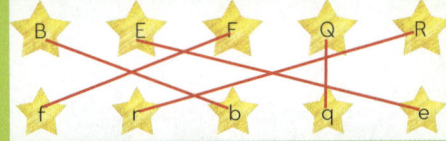

Counting Stars
The first box has 4 stars, the second box has 6 stars, and the last box has 8 stars.

Planet Patterns

Name Them All!
Circle Jupiter, Saturn, Uranus, and Neptune.

Space Suit Shapes
There are 3 circles, 1 square, 1 triangle, and 2 rectangles.

Taking a Moonwalk

Who's Coming on Board?
There are 10 lines.

Exploring the Station

pp. 94–95
Moon Words

Many Moons
There are 10 moons.
Counting Craters
There are 8 craters.

pp. 96–97
Roving Around

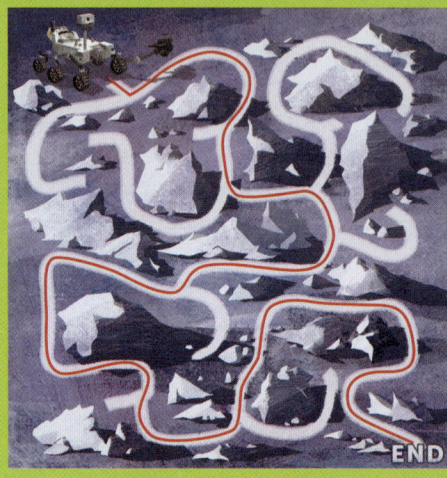

pp. 98–99
Star Search

Telescope Counting
There were 6 telescopes.
You add 4 more to get 10.

pp. 100–101
Counting Comets
There are 12 comets.

Comet Sort

pp. 102–103
Rockets Return

Safe Landing

Chapter 5: Water All Around
pp. 108–109
Do You See Water?

Match the Letters

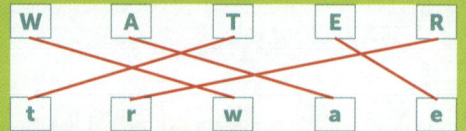

pp. 110–111
Pick the Home

Alligator's Alphabet

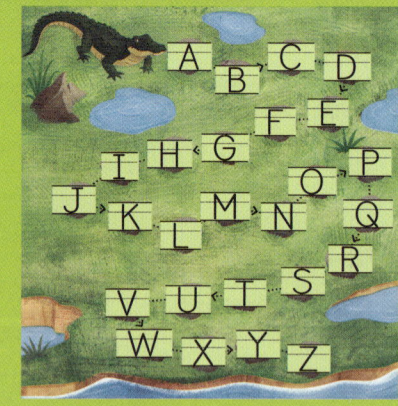

pp. 112–113
Finish the Pattern
1 and 2, respectively, come next in the pattern.

Where Can It Breathe?

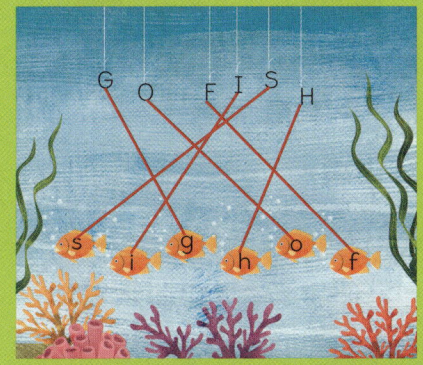

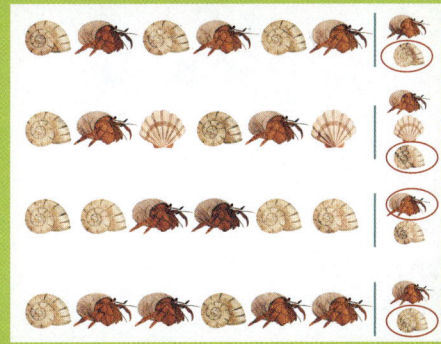
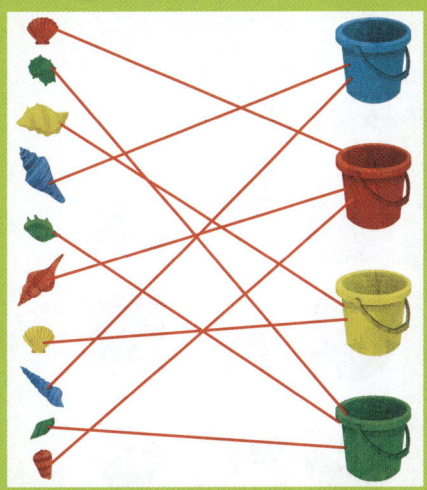

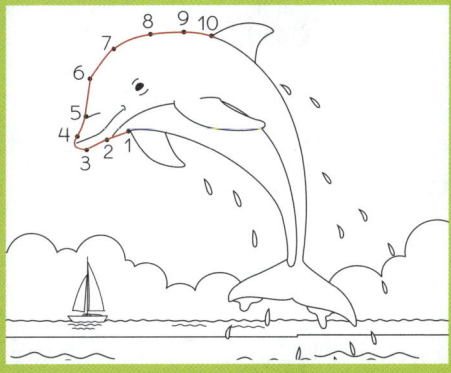

pp. 136–137

Pick the Letters

Whose Fur Is It?

pp. 138–139

Catch Up!

pp. 140–141

Always Together

There are 4 lions, 7 dolphins, and 9 wolves.

pp. 142–143

Big and Little

Bark! Bark!

pp. 144–145

Counting Chimps

There are 8 chimps.

Finding Home!

pp. 146–147

Whale Sounds

Circle the wheel.

Whale of a Rhyme!

"Tail" rhymes with "whale."

pp. 148–149

Whose Face Is This?

pp. 150–151

Mommy Matching

pp. 152–153

In or Out?

Hop to It

pp. 154–155

Cub Counting

There are 7 polar bear cubs.

Icy Alphabet

Caring for Mammals

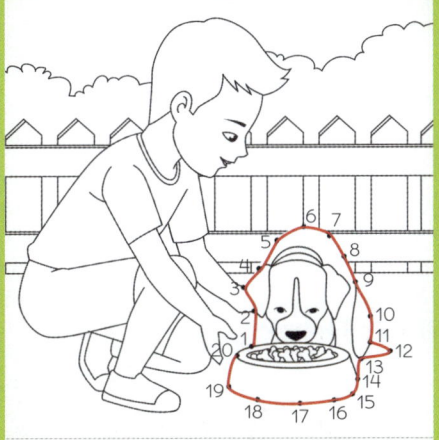

Chapter 7: In My Community

What Starts With P?

Play and Count

There are 12 benches, swings, and bikes.

On the Map

There are 8 houses.

Look for the Badge

Taller and Bigger

Stop, Drop, and Roll

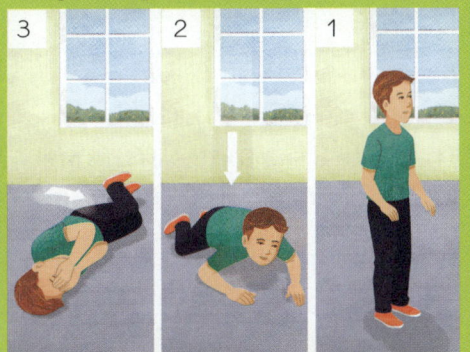

Teamwork

There are 7 firefighters.

What Starts With T?

In the Classroom

School Activities

Find the Bus!

pp. 178–179

Which Way?

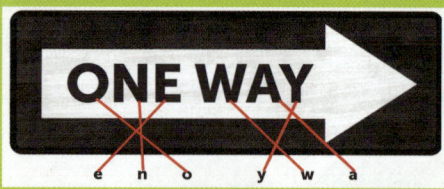

pp. 180–181

Keep Recycling!

Will It Help?

pp. 182–183

Friend Count
There are 10 friends.

Chapter 8: Home Sweet Home

pp. 188–189

Tiger Homes

pp. 190–191

Funny Faces

Desert Discovery

Desert Friends

pp. 192–193

Waddling Penguin

pp. 194–195

Totally Turtles
There are 8 sea turtles in the first group. There are 4 sea turtles in the second group.

pp. 196–197

Powerful Cats

Counting Stripes

pp. 198–199

Drips and Drops

Who's There?

pp. 200–201

Friends of the Tree

Up in the Branches
There are 10 bees.

pp. 202–203
Welcome, Babies

Uppercase Eggs

Who's Home?
The squirrel made the nest.

pp. 204–205
The Sound of B
Circle the banana, boat, and ball.
Burrowing Buddies
The totals in order are: 5, 3, 2, and 6.

pp. 206–207
Bat Search
There are 8 bats. Draw 2 more bats to make 10.
Growl!
There are 6 bears.

pp. 208–209
Trekking Tracks

Where Do They Live?

pp. 210–211
A Path Home

Gardens at Home

pp. 212–213
Who Lives Here?

Chapter 9: Brilliant Birds
pp. 216–217
How Many Eggs?

pp. 218–219
An Odd Bird

Color Match

pp. 220–221
Feathery Sounds
Circle the foot, fork, and fence.

pp. 222–223
Find the Letters

M		B	E
A	S		K

Long or Short?
The stork has the longest beak. The sparrow has the shortest legs.

More and More Beaks
There are 7 birds in the top half. There are 9 birds in the bottom half.

pp. 224–225
Which Footprint Comes Next?

How Many Toes?

8

pp. 226–227
Home Sweet Home

Feeding Time

pp. 228–229
Flying Letters

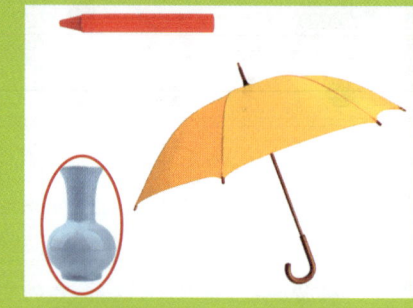

Ducky Dots

pp. 230–231
Eggy Shapes

All in Order

pp. 232–233
Matching Pals

Bird Food Counting
There are 7 worms. There are 5 seeds. There are 4 berries.

pp. 234–235
Who's the Biggest?

pp. 236–237
Pretty Parrot!
There are 6 mangoes. There are 4 bananas. There are 4 pears.

Skills Index

Use the index to find the activities that can give your child practice with math, letters, writing, reading, and early concepts such as colors, science, and sorting.

Photo Credits

COVER (chameleon illustration), Melanie Mikecz; (chameleon photo), Kuttelvaserova Stuchelova/Shutterstock; 1 (LO CTR), Kuttelvaserova Stuchelova/Shutterstock; 3 (LO), ESB Professional/Shutterstock; 3 (BACKGROUND), spacezerocom/Shutterstock

CHAPTER 1 6–7 (BACKGROUND), ondrejprosicky/Adobe Stock; 8 (UP RT), waechter-media.de/Adobe Stock; 8 (UP), grey_and/Shutterstock; 8 (CTR LE), Potapov Alexander/Shutterstock; 9 (UP LE), Africa Studio/Shutterstock; 11 (UP), shorex.koss/Shutterstock; 11 (LO CTR), Svetlana Foote/Shutterstock; 12 (UP), yod67/Adobe Stock; 12 (brown caterpillar), Jacob Tian/Adobe Stock; 12 (yellow caterpillar), Darkdiamond67/Shutterstock; 13 (UP), xpixel/Shutterstock; 14 (UP), Dee Carpenter/Adobe Stock; 15 (UP), Africa Studio/Adobe Stock; 16 (UP), Amy Lutz/Shutterstock; 18 (LO CTR), StanislauV/Shutterstock; 18 (LO RT), Shulevskyy Volodymyr/Shutterstock; 18 (LO LE), ULKASTUDIO/Shutterstock; 18 (UP RT), DmytroPerov/Shutterstock; 18, MongPro/Shutterstock; 18 (CTR), amenic181/Shutterstock; 19 (LO RT), Artiste2d3d/Shutterstock; 20 (UP), Anne Richard/Shutterstock; 22 (UP), Anan Kaewkhammul/Shutterstock; 23 (LO RT), asharkyu/Shutterstock; 24 (A), zhengchengbao/Shutterstock; 24 (B), Lemonsoup14r/Adobe Stock; 24 (C), Soru Epotok/Adobe Stock; 24 (D), TomaszPodlak/Adobe Stock; 24 (E), New Africa/Shutterstock; 24 (LO), James Casil/Shutterstock; 26 (LO), Designpics/Adobe Stock; 26 (UP LE), Anan Kaewkhammul/Shutterstock; 26 (UP CTR), Anan Kaewkhammul/Shutterstock; 26 (UP RT), Anan Kaewkhammul/Shutterstock

CHAPTER 2 30–31 (BACKGROUND), Frédéric Prochasson/Shutterstock; 32 (hay bale), gn fotografie/Shutterstock; 33 (UP CTR), VanderWolf Images/Adobe Stock; 33 (UP LE), Naurider/Shutterstock; 33 (UP RT), Inna Astakhova/Shutterstock; 33 (LO), Joanna McCarthy/Getty Images; 34 (UP RT), Emily/Adobe Stock; 34 (UP CTR), Westwood/Shutterstock; 34 (UP LE), Don Hammond/Getty Images; 34 (CTR CTR), Emily/Adobe Stock; 34 (LO RT), Don Hammond/Getty Images; 34 (LO LE), Westwood/Shutterstock; 36 (glass), ST-studio/Adobe Stock; 36 (CTR RT), Vadym Farion/Shutterstock; 38 (white egg), Maks Narodenko/Shutterstock; 38 (blue egg), Potapov Alexander/Shutterstock; 38 (pink egg),GCapture/Adobe Stock; 38 (brown egg), mayakova/Adobe Stock; 38 (brown egg in nest), picturepixx/Shutterstock; 38 (blue egg in nest), Hans Neleman/Getty Images; 38 (pink egg in nest), Susan Law Cain/Shutterstock; 39 (CTR LE), ymphotos/Shutterstock; 39 (LO LE), Patrycja Tupaj/Shutterstock; 39 (UP LE), smereka/Shutterstock; 39 (CTR RT), StockStudio Aerials/Shutterstock; 39 (LO RT), PRANEE JIRAKITDACHAKUN/Shutterstock; 39 (UP RT), Shamils/Shutterstock; 40 (shovel), AlinaMD/Shutterstock; 40 (tricycle), Tatuasha/Shutterstock; 40 (rake), ElephantCastle/Shutterstock; 40 (tractor), Photobac/Shutterstock; 40 (ball), irin-k/Shutterstock; 40 (lamp), Roman Yastrebinsky/Shutterstock; 41 (LO RT), Kasoga/Adobe Stock; 41 (LO LE), New Africa/Shutterstock; 41 (LO CTR), Spalnic/Shutterstock; 41 (UP CTR), Tim UR/Shutterstock; 41 (CTR RT), Vadym Zaitsev/Shutterstock; 41 (UP RT), Olga_i/Shutterstock; 41 (CTR LE), Shana Novak/Getty Images; 42 (LO CTR), Irina Kozorog/Shutterstock; 42 (UP), Olhastock/Shutterstock; 44 (LO), Viktoriia Kryvenko/Shutterstock; 44 (UP RT), Potapov Alexander/Shutterstock; 46 (UP LE), Tsekhmister/Shutterstock; 46 (UP RT), khathar ranglak/Shutterstock; 48 (UP RT), critterbiz/Shutterstock; 48 (LO RT), Valentina Razumova/Shutterstock; 50 (CTR RT), Production Perig/Shutterstock; 50 (CTR LE), gstalker/Shutterstock; 50 (LO LE), Studio Empreinte/Shutterstock; 50 (LO CTR), Mathisa/Shutterstock; 50 (LO RT), Butterfly Hunter/Shutterstock; 52 (UP RT), Svietlieisha Olena/Shutterstock; 53 (LO LE), Mint Images/Adobe Stock; 53 (UP RT), Designpics/Adobe Stock; 53 (LO RT), robertharding/Adobe Stock; 53 (UP LE), Rita_Kochmarjova/Shutterstock; 54 (UP RT), MaxyM/Shutterstock; 55 (LO CTR), photomaster/Shutterstock

CHAPTER 3 56–57 (BACKGROUND), Sergey Fedoskin/Adobe Stock; 58 (LO CTR), Ivonne Wierink/Shutterstock; 58 (LO CTR RT), Ievgenii Meyer/Shutterstock; 58 (LO CTR LE), azure1/Shutterstock; 58 (LO RT), Suleyman Delil Karakurt/Shutterstock; 58 (LO LE), Tatiana Popova/Shutterstock; 59 (UP RT), Milan/Adobe Stock; 60 (CTR RT), Byjeng/Shutterstock; 60 (UP CTR RT), Funny Solution Studio/Shutterstock; 60 (UP CTR), Yeti studio/Shutterstock; 60 (UP RT), Casezy idea/Shutterstock; 60 (CTR CTR), New Africa/Shutterstock; 60 (CTR LE), Jan Martin Will/Shutterstock; 60 (UP RT), irin-k/Shutterstock; 62 (UP CTR RT), Jennifer Princ/Shutterstock; 62 (UP RT), Jan Day/Shutterstock; 65 (LO RT), LeManna/Shutterstock; 65 (LO CTR), OlgaGir/Shutterstock; 65 (CTR LE), Ruslan Kudrin/Shutterstock; 65 (UP CTR RT), LeManna/Shutterstock; 65 (UP CTR LE), Pixel-Shot/Shutterstock; 65 (UP RT), Sergey Novikov/Shutterstock; 65 (LO LE), Tatiana Popova/Shutterstock; 65 (LO CTR RT), ND700/Shutterstock; 66 (UP RT), Takacs Szabolcs/Shutterstock; 68 (UP), Smit/Shutterstock; 68 (LO CTR RT), Paul Orr/Shutterstock; 69 (UP RT), ksena32/Adobe Stock; 69 (LO CTR), Africa Studio/Shutterstock; 70 (CTR RT), Peter Bocklandt/Shutterstock; 70 (CTR), mykhailo pavlenko/Shutterstock; 70 (RT), FamVeld/Shutterstock; 70 (CTR LE), SUN IMAGE/Shutterstock; 70 (UP RT), 19 STUDIO/Shutterstock; 71 (UP RT), Pilith/Shutterstock; 71 (CTR RT), avs/Shutterstock; 71 (LO LE), Gena73/Shutterstock; 71 (CTR LE), KawaiiS/Shutterstock; 71 (LO RT), Timmary/Shutterstock; 72 (CTR RT), Andrey Solovev/Shutterstock; 72 (UP RT), Alexey Kljatov/Shutterstock; 73 (UP RT), Alexey Kljatov/Shutterstock; 74 (UP), vovan/Shutterstock; 74 (LO LE), Krakenimages/Shutterstock; 74 (LO RT), Krakenimages/Shutterstock; 74 (LO CTR), 2xSamara/Shutterstock; 74 (CTR RT), KK Tan/Shutterstock; 76 (UP LE), jakkrapong wangkiree/Adobe Stock; 76 (UP CTR), CE Photography/Shutterstock; 76 (CTR RT), John D Sirlin/Shutterstock; 76 (UP RT), Phattaraphum/Shutterstock; 78 (UP), Dmitry Naumov/Adobe Stock; 79 (UP RT), Ruslan Ivantsov/Shutterstock; 80 (UP RT), Svitlana Kataieva/Shutterstock; 81 (UP RT), FaridAlili/Shutterstock

CHAPTER 4 82–83 (BACKGROUND), Merrillie Redden/Shutterstock; 82 (LO CTR LE), Dotted Yeti/Shutterstock; 85 (CTR), wowinside/Adobe Stock; 88–89 (planets), 19 STUDIO/Shutterstock; 88–89 (Uranus), wasan/Adobe Stock; 90 (UP RT), Andrei Armiagov/Shutterstock; 92 (astronaut), M.Aurelius/Shutterstock; 92 (CTR), Dima Zel/Shutterstock; 93 (UP RT), Alstudio1/Adobe Stock; 94 (crescent moon), Sergey Nivens/Shutterstock; 94 (milk), Hurst Photo/Shutterstock; 94 (mop), anmbph/Shutterstock; 94 (mouse), EgoreichenkovEvgenii/Shutterstock; 94 (shirt), Olga Pink/Shutterstock; 94 (Jupiter moon), Elena11/Shutterstock; 94 (footprint), NASA/Shutterstock; 95 (UP RT), Daniel Fung/Shutterstock; 96 (UP RT), Dima Zel/Shutterstock; 98 (UP RT), frantic00/Shutterstock; 99 (telescope), tomeqs/Shutterstock; 100 (UP RT), Marko Aliaksandr/Shutterstock; 100, Triff/Shutterstock; 101 (CTR RT), Lukasz Pawel Szczepanski/Shutterstock; 101 (UP LE), Elena11/Shutterstock; 101 (UP CTR), Thomas Roell/Shutterstock; 101 (UP RT), Photoongraphy/Shutterstock; 101 (CTR CTR), NASA images/Shutterstock; 101 (CTR LE), berrydog/Shutterstock; 101 (LO RT), robert_s/Shutterstock; 101 (LO LE), solarseven/Shutterstock; 101 (LO CTR), Triff/Shutterstock; 104 (UP LE), Dan Thornberg/Shutterstock; 104 (CTR), Juergen Faelchle/Shutterstock

CHAPTER 5 106–107 (BACKGROUND), Kelly Headrick/Shutterstock; 108 (CTR LE), Kenneth Keifer/Adobe Stock; 108 (LO RT), jonbilous/Adobe Stock; 108 (CTR RT), fastudio4/Adobe Stock; 108 (UP RT), Irina Markova/Shutterstock; 108 (LO LE), Aleksandr Ozerov/Shutterstock; 108 (UP LE), Bilanol/Shutterstock; 109, Dmitry Gritsenko/Shutterstock; 110 (UP CTR LE), Ayan/Adobe Stock; 110 (CTR RT), PNG STORE/Adobe Stock; 110 (CTR LE), natara/Adobe Stock; 110 (UP CTR RT), Eric Isselée/Adobe Stock; 110 (CTR CTR), Henner Damke/Adobe Stock; 110 (RT), DRPLr/Adobe Stock; 110 (LO CTR), Eric Isselee/Shutterstock; 110 (LE), Romolo Tavani/Shutterstock; 110 (UP RT), Anneka/Shutterstock; 112 (LO), tab62/Adobe Stock; 112 (UP), Henrik A. Jonsson/Shutterstock; 113 (UP CTR LE), Odua Images/Adobe Stock; 113 (LO CTR), alphaspirit/Adobe Stock; 113 (CTR RT), Rich Carey/Shutterstock; 113 (LO LE), Gualberto Becerra/Shutterstock; 113 (UP LE), MR. SUWIT GAEWSEE-NGAM/Shutterstock; 113 (UP RT), Alexia Khruscheva/Shutterstock; 114 (UP RT), yoshimi maeda/Shutterstock; 115 (UP RT), vnlit/Adobe Stock; 116 (UP RT), VO IMAGES/Shutterstock; 117 (LO CTR LE), cobaltstock/Adobe Stock; 118 (UP RT), PhotoSpirit/Adobe Stock; 120 (UP LE), Yevhenii Chulovskyi/Shutterstock; 120 (UP RT), Mariusz Blach/Adobe Stock; 120 (LO LE), amadeustx/Adobe Stock; 120 (LO RT), kavram/Shutterstock; 121 (UP CTR), Andrew Mayovskyy/Adobe Stock; 121 (CTR RT), ESB Professional/Shutterstock; 121 (CTR CTR), worldclassphoto/Shutterstock; 121 (UP RT), Maridav/Shutterstock; 122 (CTR RT), Ryan Janssens/Shutterstock; 124 (UP RT), Agus Gatam/Adobe Stock; 125 (UP RT), Nata Vakorina/Adobe Stock; 126 (UP RT), Neil Bromhall/Shutterstock; 129 (LO RT), pan demin/Shutterstock; 130 (UP RT), Ziga Camernik/Shutterstock; 131 (UP RT), FedBul/Shutterstock

CHAPTER 6 132–133 (BACKGROUND), phototrip.cz/Adobe Stock; 134 (UP LE), Pearl-diver/Shutterstock; 134 (UP RT), Finpat/Shutterstock; 135 (A), Dr.Pixel/Shutterstock; 135 (B), Farinoza/Adobe Stock; 135 (C), Vladfotograf/Shutterstock; 135 (D), Michael/Adobe Stock; 135 (E), Utekhina Anna/Shutterstock; 135 (F), Eric Isselee/Shutterstock; 135 (G), ESB Professional/Shutterstock; 135 (H), Eric Isselee/Shutterstock; 135 (I), SUPIDA KHEMAWAN/Shutterstock; 135 (J), Chris Willemsen/Adobe Stock; 136 (UP), Designpics/Adobe Stock; 136 (CTR RT), Yoshinori Miyazaki/Wirestock Creators/Adobe Stock; 137 (A), dangdumrong/Shutterstock; 137 (B), Puttachat Kumkrong/Shutterstock; 137 (C), Eric Isselee/Shutterstock; 137 (D), TigerStocks/Shutterstock; 137 (E), volkova natalia/Shutterstock; 137 (F), Eric Isselee/Shutterstock; 137 (G), RAJU SONI/Shutterstock; 137 (H), Eric Isselee/Shutterstock; 137 (I), Eric Isselée/Shutterstock; 137 (J), LittlePerfectStock/Shutterstock; 137 (K), ericlefrancais/Shutterstock; 137 (L), sermiyalla/Shutterstock; 138 (CTR LE), Gaston Piccinetti/Shutterstock; 138 (UP RT), WildMedia/Shutterstock; 138 (LO RT), Darren Baker/Shutterstock; 139 (UP RT), robertharding/Adobe Stock; 140 (wolf), PixelMaster/Shutterstock; 140 (dolphin), Potapov Alexander/Shutterstock; 140 (lioness), Eric Isselee/Shutterstock; 141 (UP RT), divedog/Adobe Stock; 141 (CTR LE), Designpics/Adobe Stock; 141 (LO LE), motorolka/Shutterstock; 141 (CTR RT), Laurinson Crusoe/Shutterstock; 141 (UP LE), Cat Bell/Shutterstock; 144 (LO), Edwin Butter/Shutterstock; 144 (chimpanzee), Mario Plechaty Photograph/Shutterstock; 146 (LO CTR), Christian Delbert/Shutterstock; 146 (LO RT), Feng Yu/Shutterstock; 146 (LO LE), LucyLooLoo/Shutterstock; 146 (UP RT), Doptis/Shutterstock; 146 (UP LE), Doc White/Nature Picture Library; 147 (whale), Todd Winner/Adobe Stock; 148 (UP LE), Tatiana/Adobe Stock; 148 (UP RT), gilitukha/Adobe Stock; 149 (UP CTR), ashva/Adobe Stock; 149 (CTR RT), David/Adobe Stock; 149 (LO RT), apple2499/Shutterstock; 149 (LO LE), Drakuliren/Shutterstock; 149 (UP RT), Benny Marty/Shutterstock; 149 (CTR CTR), photomaster/Shutterstock; 149 (UP LE), ashva/Adobe Stock; 149 (CTR LE), David/Adobe Stock; 149 (LO CTR), Drakuliren/Shutterstock; 150 (LO), shpock/Adobe Stock; 150 (UP), Ghost Bear/Shutterstock; 150 (CTR), Holly Kuchera/Shutterstock; 151 (UP), Oleksandr Lytvynenko/Shutterstock; 151 (LE A), Xyo/Shutterstock; 151 (LE B), Eric Isselee/Shutterstock; 151 (LE C), Leo Lintang/Adobe Stock; 151 (LE D), ChameleonsEye/Shutterstock; 151 (RT A), Eric Isselee/Shutterstock; 151 (RT B), ErmolaevAlexandr/AdobeStock; 151 (RT C), Eric Isselée/Adobe Stock; 151 (RT D), Eric Isselee/Shutterstock; 152 (UP LE), IntoTheWorld/Shutterstock; 152 (UP CTR), Wonderly Imaging/Shutterstock; 152 (UP RT), idiz/Shutterstock; 152 (LO LE), worldswildlifewonders/Shutterstock; 152 (LO RT), John Carnemolla/Shutterstock; 153 (UP RT), alybaba/Shutterstock; 153 (LO LE), Andrew AtkinsonShutterstock; 153 (CTR LE), Martin Koebsch/Shutterstock; 153 (CTR RT), karenfoleyphotography/Shutterstock; 153 (UP LE), Sandra Chia/Shutterstock; 153 (LO RT), Sandra Chia/Shutterstock; 154 (UP RT), isabel kendzior/Shutterstock; 154 (polar bear), GTW/Shutterstock; 156 (UP), Karen Grigoryan/Shutterstock;

Thinking About School

Draw a picture of yourself in school.

What would you most like to do while you are there?

NATIONAL GEOGRAPHIC KiDS

Turn the page for your Explorer Award!

Explorer Award

Great job!

You learned all about the wide world around you. You are ready for an amazing adventure!

This award goes to:

Write your name on the line.